# THE COUNTESS AND THE MOB

# THE COUNTESS AND THE MOB

The untold story of Marajen Stevick
Chinigo and Mafia lord Johnny Rosselli

*Maureen Hughes*

iUniverse, Inc.
New York   Bloomington

iUniverse books may be ordered through booksellers or by contacting:

iUniverse
1663 Liberty Drive
Bloomington, IN 47403
www.iuniverse.com
1-800-Authors (1-800-288-4677)

Because of the dynamic nature of the Internet, any Web addresses or links
contained in this book may have changed since publication and may no longer be
valid. The views expressed in this work are solely those of the author and do not
necessarily reflect the views of the publisher, and the publisher hereby disclaims
any responsibility for them.

ISBN: 978-1-4502-0750-8 (sc)
ISBN: 978-1-4502-0748-5 (hc)
ISBN: 978-1-4502-0749-2 (ebook)

Library of Congress Control Number: 2010901927

Printed in the United States of America

iUniverse rev. date: 03/05/2010

# Acknowledgments

**Special thanks to:**

Barbara Main, Bayard Stockton, and Henry Sansone Jr.

**With appreciation**

Joe McNamara, Lisa Birch, Bobby Eisner, "Star," "T," "Jim," Kyle Robinson, Professor Michele Ingento, Mrs. Joe Wambaugh, the family of Greta Alexander, former soap opera star Dena Ivancie, and actress Ms. Barbara Parsons.

# Author's note

To those I owe more than thanks:

Finding a way to sufficiently thank those who have opened their homes, their memories, and their hearts is harder to do than it was to write this book. Many of Marajen's friends wrote long, emotional letters to me. Most added humorous quips about their relationship with her. Others told specific stories of either a social event where Marajen was present or a business connection they had with her. Former employees told of a different side of Marajen that few of us knew or witnessed. Still others agreed to talk with me only with a partition between us or on a pay phone, and one even spoke in a disguised voice.

To the long-time residents of Champaign, Illinois, who sat back in easy chairs on patios in the summer or in front of fireplaces as blowing snow formed moguls under winter living room windows, and educated me on the "early days" of Champaign—I give my thanks to each and every one of you for your time and contributions. A very special thanks to Barbara Main, who considered Marajen a sister. Barbara's warm personality and gracious acceptance of my goal in writing this book has been an enormous help when I had questions or concerns about the colorful Marajen Stevick Chinigo. I also wish to thank the late Bayard Stockton, a former G-man, for being there for me in assisting me in gaining access to government records for the research part of this book. Bayard was my friend and mentor, and any student who studied under him would agree he was a tough teacher. Finally, I wish to thank my family, who have put up with "I'll be late for supper" phone calls and quick trips to the West Coast; I also appreciate their tolerance when I was deep in thought.

# *Prologue*

My introduction to Marajen Chinigo came in the 1980s as she was being admitted to the Carle Foundation Hospital in Champaign, Illinois. She was there to be diagnosed for what were believed to be blood clots in her legs, and she would be there a couple of days. My job as her personal security person, was to stay with her 24/7 if need be and insure that only authorized people were admitted to her room.

I knew very little about her, other than she was a VIP in Champaign; I heard the word Countess used when she was addressed by the medical staff. As she was being helped into bed a tall, thin man in a suit arrived and sat outside her door. I never knew his name, and he never asked for mine.

Eventually, I managed to engage her in conversation about her hospital room, which she described as "classically medical." "It's no wonder people die here! Bland gray and dull blue walls to stare at," she said. Later she stated that she was the owner and publisher of the News-Gazette newspaper, and she had a villa in Italy, where she wished she was now.

Once her supper tray was removed, a nurse set a small white paper cup with her night medications on her nightstand and left. I asked if she would like more ice water, and she asked if

I had anything stronger to drink. With that she chuckled and pulled the covers under her chin.

Thinking she wanted to sleep, I went to the nightstand to turn out the light. Marajen shot up in her bed and told me to get away from the light. "I want it on, do you hear?" This was a flashback for me; I was afraid of the dark because of the eerie shadows that danced on my bedroom window at night. But I was five years old. "I want the light left on all the time. I don't want you leaving me alone in here, either, do you hear?" Seeing the anxious expression on her face, I asked if I could do anything to make her more comfortable.

Almost in a whisper she said, "Just get the demons away from me and I will be happy." Steering the conversation to a more pleasant subject, I asked about her home in Italy.

She spoke of its history and the beautiful scenery around it, which she had painted on canvas. She spoke of her parents, who had started the newspaper and the two radio stations in Champaign.

Within an hour she was asleep and looked comfortable. I sat in the La-Z-Boy chair across the room and opened a book to read. In the early hours of morning Marajen began talking in her sleep. "Johnny," she said, "Where are you? I can't see you. Johnny? Johnny? What did you do to Michael?"

A few years later I would see Marajen again, on a social level. Her paintings were being displayed at the Krannert Museum of Fine Arts at the University of Illinois. Though she didn't see me, I observed for myself what a charming woman she was. Impeccably dressed and with perfectly styled hair, she strolled through the crowd like a queen, calling everyone by their first name, followed by a little quip that pertained to them. Marajen Chinigo was, indeed, the hostess to be remembered.

At the art exhibit, I spoke with a man who had known Marajen for many years. He said she was born with a silver spoon in her mouth. She had looks, wealth, and a name that would command attention. She craved the glamour, the glitz, and the power that the rich and famous had. As the exhibit prepared to wind down, we carried the conversation to a local bar in Champaign. At the close of the evening I vowed to find out all I could about this somewhat mysterious woman. The journey was long, and I found myself in the dark crevices of people's memories.

Behind the charm and polish the public saw and the romantic aspects of high society she displayed on the outside, there was a dark and cynical side of the newspaper heiress.

The three-plus years I spent researching this book allowed me to meet many people I otherwise would not have. Most of them, friends of Marajen Chinigo, I spoke with over the phone for hours or communicated with by letter. Others invited me into their homes and reminisced about their lives and their connections with Marajen. On the darker side, a small group agreed to talk with me under the agreement that their names not be used. Through their candor I was able to answer some of my own questions and confirm my suspicions about Marajen.

On two occasions I was in contact with two professional guns. Neither of them showed their faces nor gave a name. In our conversations I saw a side of them that their victims never knew, a human, caring side garnished with a sense of humor. Both expressed respect for me for obtaining the information I sought their way. To my regret, a few profoundly informative people have passed on. However, their memories are recorded now and can be reviewed by those who read this account.

Within the following pages are the kaleidoscopic shapes and colors that made up Countess Marajen Stevick Chinigo.

# A Little Bit of History

Marajen Stevick Chinigo was raised during a period of time when glamour and glitz were just dreams to small-town girls in the Midwest. Champaign, Illinois, a typical Midwestern town, offered a solid foundation for any dreamy-eyed young girl during the early 1900s. But Champaign was a stubborn community bent on being more than a whistle stop. Marajen Stevick Chinigo, born with the same pernicious grit, was not going to be lost in the back pages of history books.

It is important to visualize a panoramic picture of Illinois and how the state coalesced through inexorable efforts and, yes, sometimes crime, to become the state it is. Illinois' infancy held a lot of surprises for those heading west. Champaign did not grow as rapidly as other budding towns because it had been labeled a malaria area. Pioneer settlers found the flat, grassy terrain hard to adjust to after leaving the East's bountiful mountains and timbers. President James Monroe, after only two visits, eagerly released the prairie territory from Virginia because, as he put it, the land was miserably poor. But the pioneers continued to come, bringing new ideas, new techniques and methods and new diseases. Cases of malaria kept the population down, and physicians were hesitant to begin a practice in Champaign. Only after the Illinois Central

Railroad arrived did the community of Champaign take root. In 1860 the population of Champaign was large enough to be incorporated. Due to its growth, General Grant was able to draw a sizeable military company from Champaign County for service in the Civil War.[1]

Newcomers settling in Champaign were immigrants or children of immigrants who had walked through the gates of Ellis Island. They were of German, Irish, or Italian heritage. Once on the shores of New York City, some stayed a few years and then moved westward to more promising cities such as Chicago. Others moved to smaller, quieter communities to continue to do what their families had done for centuries: farm. In 1867 the promising bedroom community in central Illinois was busy becoming a university town, specializing in agricultural and industry. Times were hard, and making a living in town was even harder. If not farming or retail, most Germans worked in the beer breweries, Italians made wines, from the Irish made whiskey.

While homes were being made and schools being filled with youngsters who struggled to drop their native accents, a quiet but prominent group of people were busy working on new legislation that would alter history and add a new amendment to the seventeen that made up our Constitution: the abolition of alcohol.

The war on alcohol was not new; in fact, was at least a century old. It came across with the Mayflower. Native Americans traded fish, furs, and crop farming knowledge for alcohol. As history writes, this proved devastating to the Native American nations and their future. Women's groups, with the backing of the ministries, were fighting for moderation or abstinence of alcohol indulgence. Had the media been then what it is today, the Midwest would have crammed the headlines of the press. Carry Nation, a Kansas native and the object of abuse as a result of alcohol, was hell-bent on stopping the sale and consumption of alcohol and became a storm trooper in stopping the building of saloons. She and her followers covered the Midwest, terrorizing taverns and destroying what they could with hatchets. Her techniques failed, but she kept the dream of a non-alcoholic society very much alive.

In 1914 WWI drew the attention of the nation in a different direction for a different cause. Germany was now the enemy. Literature by the German masters was destroyed. Universities released German professors, and German curriculum was abolished from American institutions of higher education.

Wayne Wheeler of Ohio was recruited by Washington's politicians as a lobbyist to form the Anti-Saloon League, an anti-alcohol organization. Powerful names like the Rockefellers, the DuPonts, and the Henry Ford family financed Wheeler's propaganda on Capitol Hill. The fear was that German breweries in America aided the German government, the American enemy. It was felt that materials used in the beer-making process could be better used to support our troops in uniform. In 1919 the prohibition of alcohol became the Eighteenth Amendment. One midnight in January 1920, taverns were to be closed. The Internal Revenue Service was given the sole authority to see that the amendment was enforced.

This snag in the legitimate booze business opened the cellar door to the already entrenched underground business of bootlegging.

What had originally been a personal supply of booze produced in basements and stills on the farms suddenly became an overnight monetary windfall. Southern Illinois became infested with backwoods stills. Root cellars in the urban areas of the state now stored more than just potatoes. Prohibition didn't stop the power of booze, but it did stop the skimming of revenue from previously legitimate saloon owners in large metropolises by another organization closer than Capitol Hill.

The Detroit River became the epicenter for illegal booze traffic during Prohibition. Canada, seeing a financial market in the United States, modified their liquor laws to allow the production of rum for export sales only. Ships brought rum to the doorway of Detroit, where idling trucks waited to take it to smaller boats under the guise of legal imported products. In the winter months, cars and trucks drove across the frozen river to be loaded and driven back. To carry more rum, Model Ts would pull short flatbeds to the waiting boats. After the cargo was loaded, the trip back began. Late winter posed a problem due to thinner ice. But daredevils seeing the dollar signs would take the risk. Many cars and flatbeds loaded with rum found their way to the bottom of the Detroit River as a result of taking that risk. The successful drivers maneuvered their cargo down the river to the banks of Lake Michigan, into Chicago.

# Chicago's Families Gain Control of the Booze Industry

The world of gangs is believed confined to cities like New York, Chicago, and Las Vegas. Hollywood used Boston and Chicago as the templates for mafia strongholds. It's true the outfits were entrenched in those cities. They cut their teeth there and built their empires in the ethnic neighborhoods. Ask anyone what Chicago is known for and they will likely say Caponeland. Al Capone, the pudgy, bullheaded muscle man from New York became John Torrio's gun man in Chicago around 1920. Torrio was a straight-shooter mobster enjoying the profits of the vices he ruled. Wanting command of the Chicago territory, Torrio gave Capone the order to whack top-level mobster Big Jim Colosimo while Big Jim was engaged in a rendezvous with a nightclub singer. Torrio had now established a place in the Chicago Syndicate. He realized that bootlegging was the source of a handsome income, and he didn't miss a beat with Prohibition. He became fearless with power, and he had Capone for his muscle. Liking the Windy City and proving his worth in the business, Capone began to build his empire shortly after Torrio was severely wounded in 1925.

Earning the reputation he sought with the Chicago Family,

Al Capone wedged his way among the social clientele as a bouncer in an underground bar. During his shift one night he made the mistake of telling a female patron that she "had a nice ass." The brother of the woman, hearing what Capone had said, pushed Capone against a wall and tried to cut his throat. Missing the target, the knife left an ugly line down Al's left cheek. From then on Al Capone's nickname was Scarface.

Cities north and south of Chicago were feeling the effects of a dry nation. Quick-thinking gangsters, like the up-and-coming Dion O'Banion on Chicago's north side, hijacked a truckload of Irish whiskey in preparation for the New Year's festivities. Other thefts occurred as shipments of booze entered the city. O'Banion knew he could reap top dollar for a nip, so the stockpile was split between Chicago, Cicero, Joliet, Waukegan, and Champaign. Ambitious daredevils offered to transport booze up to Milwaukee and down to Champaign.

Brewery and tavern signs came down at the beginning of Prohibition, and fake storefront names sprang up. Those wanting to drink were given a code; if the customer spoke softly, the store owner would let him into a back room where the illegal beer and rum was stocked. Supplying the ever-growing number of speak-easies in Chicago offered a good income, but other cities hankered for the sparsely available booze, and that meant an even bigger income from down-state. At night Route 45 south became the main road for the Chicago-to-Champaign liquor delivery. Nights when a full moon was out, cars and trucks loaded with booze would drive bumper to bumper, as there was no need for lights.

With the hype on the big cities, little was said about the rest of Illinois and the role the outfit played down-state. The Prohibition era didn't just affect Chicago. Small towns like Champaign felt the pinch the same way. People weren't going to stop drinking just because the law said to. They were even willing to pay the going price, which in many places increased from ten or fifteen cents to almost $3 in the larger cities. Many of Champaign's noted families, such as Robeson and Davis, helped keep Champaign "wet" during Prohibition. It kept some change in their pockets and food on the table. Another name connected with Champaign was Sansone.

Born in Sicily, the Sansone family immigrated to America through Ellis Island and went on to Champaign. Finding ways to support a family of eleven children was a daily chore. Jobs were scarce, but the Sansone sons did what they could to bring an income into the household. Michael Sansone purchased vending machines that made taffy. His concession stand, a big hit at the county fair in the summers, was kept at Crystal Lake. Henry Sansone operated a popcorn wagon that became an icon on Champaign streets for decades. Though an honest living, it earned barely enough to keep the family's head above water. From dawn to dusk Henry stood on the street corner by the Virginia Theater selling popcorn to shoppers, retailers, and local attorneys. Julius Hirshfeld, a credible and distinguished attorney in Champaign, was one of Henry's regular customers. Julius spent time with Henry, standing on the street corner chatting about current events, the weather, and neighborhood gossip. It wasn't long before they became good friends. Julius learned that Henry was an avid hunter, and when the Hirshfelds hosted formal dinners for statesmen from Springfield and other attorneys, Julius would call on Henry to supply the meat for the dinner. Henry would do the honors, supplying ducks for $3, pheasants for $5, and rabbits for 50 cents each. News traveled north about the fine dining that Henry Sansone could provide, and it wasn't long before a couple of Capone's down-state lieutenants heard about the hunting south of Champaign. Capone asked if Henry could set up a hunting trip for "the boys." This was no problem, and for the next three to four years Henry had Capone's outfit come out of the city for some good pheasant and duck hunting. In return, Capone would provide Sansone a roll of cash at the end of the day. And they were good days, when everyone could forget their station in life and just be guys out hunting. Henry realized that setting up hunting trips could be quite lucrative and decide to expand his hunting schedule to include George "Bugs" Moran, an enemy of Capone.

This shouldn't have been a problem. Sansone scheduled Moran and his boys on opposite weekends from when Capone was down. This would have worked well, except the scheduling was done by word of mouth, and one weekend the dates got mixed up. One particular Saturday when Bugsy Moran was hunting, three black cars pulled up two hours later, and five men got out, including Al Capone. Everyone was dressed in hunting gear, so it was hard to positively identify anyone. By mid-morning, the men from both gangs were just two or three hundred feet apart when one of Capone's men asked why Moran was there. That's all it took for the shooting to start. Both gangs retreated to their cars, and several had to lie in the back seats all the way to Chicago because they had lead shot in their rear ends. So ended the hunting trips to Champaign.

Several years later, Henry would call on Julius Hirshfeld's expertise in a civil case being tried in Champaign County. When parking meters became a source of city revenue, neighboring retailers noticed that Henry Sansone wasn't paying the meter where he had his popcorn wagon parked. Their ire raised the local retailers' banded together and filed suit against Henry. A family man with meager financial resources, Henry consulted Julius Hirshfeld over the suit. Julius and another well-established attorney known as JJ, who incidentally was blind, advised Henry from the sidelines at no expense to Sansone. As the trial dragged on, the Chicago papers covered the unusual case and published the continuing saga in the first section. The headlines condemned the local retailers who had filed the suit by making them out to be silly hicks. Sansone represented himself and won the case. The newspapers, local and in Chicago, ran the bold print: **"He fought the city and won!"** Henry Sansone went on to sell popcorn from his wagon for several more years, until the wagon was sold in 1962.

Frank, another Sansone son, tired of his poor standard of living, ventured out in search of a better way of making a living in the early 1930s. A businessman with dreams of earning big money, Frank found his way to Chicago.

In the town of Cicero, Frank met Frank Milano, a low-level Mafiosi, who needed a driver to make beer deliveries to down-state merchants. The fast-talking Milano took Frank to the back door of a bar in Cicero to get the approval of the boss. In the doorway stood a man in an expensive suit with a cigar in his mouth. "This is the kid, Al!" Milano said. The stocky man in the doorway chewed on his cigar awhile and asked Frank if he had a car. Frank, who was driving a Model T, nodded yes and soon became a driver for none other than Al Capone.

The trip to Cicero two or three times a week added to the family income and provided the kids with acceptable clothing. When Frank returned to Champaign with the crates of booze, his mother and younger brothers would hide the crates in the boys' bedroom until the contraband was needed in local taverns and those as far away as Bloomington and Peoria.

Johnny Sansone operated a whiskey package house behind the old News-Gazette's location. Johnny and Frank had a good business going with the North End taverns in Champaign. Supplying booze from Chicago to black-operated taverns and backroom gambling houses was so easy they could have made their clandestine booze deliveries in broad daylight. At night cops sitting in squad cars parked down from the taverns would watch Johnny and Frank pull in the alley to make the scheduled delivery. Never did law enforcement stop the brothers or check to see what the delivery was. There was good reason for this. Champaign police chief Clyde Davis had a stake in the enterprise. Once a week Clyde would pull up in front of the taverns and get out of the car carrying a thin, worn satchel. A short time later he would reappear with a fat and heavy satchel.

The contents of the fat satchel were the tavern owner's tokens of appreciation for not being busted for illegal booze. Chief Davis kept the lid on crime in Champaign, and the riffraff that accompanied it, by sharing in the wealth.

While Frank and Johnny ran the booze, younger brother Joseph was involved in race cars and gambling in the back room of his business. Gambling was a constant form of entertainment and false dreams in the whiskey packaging house behind the old News-Gazette. The second floor held poker tables and slot machines that rarely gathered dust. Vriner's Confectionary served sandwiches—until the wives figured out what was going on and notified the police. The gambling parlor was busted and buried. [2]

Needing more drivers for the Chicago to Champaign route, Frank Sansone enticed friend George Meyer to participate. Meyer, born to German parents in the small town of Monticello, Illinois, twenty miles from Champaign, became one of Capone's youngest and fastest drivers. Nicknamed Devil by Frank Nitti, Meyer was Capone's favorite driver. The one infamous act that George Meyer would never get credit for was being the wheelman at the St. Valentine's Day Massacre on February 14, 1929. George was never charged with, nor tried for, the crime and only looked away when asked about it. The black Cadillac that Meyer drove was found February 29, 1929, in a garage at 1723 North Wood Street. The garage had been torched after the Cadillac was demolished with an acetylene torch and hacksaw.

While newspapers coast to coast covered the grizzly event, Capone had left his headquarters at 2300 S. Michigan Avenue for his home in Florida.

After laying low for weeks Frank Sansone and George Meyer continued to rule the highway for Capone's beer supply trucks for $500 each every week. George Meyer admitted that the booze business only brought the worst out in gangsters. Gang war killings among rival mobsters became commonplace.

If alcohol brought the cash in, then Mob violence served as the jury to see who collected the revenue.

Because George was not Italian he couldn't become part of the "family," but he remained a crucial part of the link in the syndicate's activities between Chicago and Champaign. The oddity in the relationship between George Meyer and the Chicago outfit was that Meyer was probably one of the few gangsters who had a conscience.

I spoke with Meyer when he was part of the prison ministries. He recalled one incident that bothered him to his dying day. He was ordered to drive to Champaign on a business trip. Two men rode in the back seat. Meyer was ordered not to turn around. He obeyed. Meyer drove west of Champaign on Route 10 past Anderson's Grain Elevator into a cornfield. The two men in the back got out of the car and walked farther into the field. Shortly after, George Meyer heard a gun blast, and then only one man returned to the car. Not a word was said during the trip back to Chicago.

Another story told was that in the '70s, the Ramada Inn in Champaign had one outstanding characteristic over all the other Ramada Inns. The hotel ran in the black. According to George Meyer, Mob money from the Chicago family was laundered through it. Known by the Mob as a setup man as well as a trusted driver, Meyer arranged for a high stakes poker game to be held in a specific room on a specific floor. A couple of boys from Florida would be playing with members of the Chicago family. One of the players was an attorney for the Chicago Mob. Meyer believed this was intended to be more than just a poker game. The Chicago Mob owed George money for work he had done for them, and payment was long overdue. He suspected the new names in the Chicago family wanted to cleanse the family of old Capone members and sending down a man to remove Meyer was part of the purpose he suspected. Meyer made excuses for not attending the poker game and made other arrangements for his payoff. A few days later Meyer called the Mob attorney and had the drop scheduled in an alley behind Charles Street in Champaign. From a second story window Meyer watched a car approach; a man opened the passenger door and laid a bag in the alley. Once the bag was dropped, the car left. After several minutes George ventured down to the alley and retrieved his pay.

Becoming known and liked by Capone, Frank Sansone began to rise in the family. Little has been documented about what Frank's new responsibilities were, but it is known that he became a made man in Capone's syndicate, though he was never involved in any killings. He proved his worth in other ways.

Frank Robeson of Champaign also delivered Capone booze to Champaign. In those days it wasn't frowned upon, as it put food on the table. Being conservative with his income, Frank started what was to become Robeson's Department Store, which lasted for decades. Before Prohibition was lifted, countless families in downstate Illinois benefited financially from the Eighteenth Amendment—families that today still remain in Champaign and have contributed much to the growth and prosperity of the booming town.[3]

# The Newspaper Business

Building a successful, dominating newspaper doesn't come easy. The Chicago Tribune bullied its way into becoming a leading newspaper using Mob connections as far back as the early 1900s. In the early days Chicago could boast upwards of ten newspapers, plus a William R. Hearst paper. Tribune stockholders with powerful names such as Rockefeller and Field backed the threat of revenge on competing circulation departments. Mentioning Mr. Field or Mr. Rockerfeller often scared the competition away. When verbal threats didn't succeed, more direct action was taken to get the attention of the competition. Vehicles used to carry the Tribune throughout the city and elsewhere carried armed sluggers aboard to shoot at the vehicles carrying copies of competing newspapers. The problem was that the shootings often took place when the streets of Chicago were filled with innocent bystanders and people walking to work. Many were maimed or killed. This, of course, didn't set well with the police or public. To correct the problem, the Tribune secured the services of the Annenberg family, better known as the Junkyard Kings. Moses Annenberg was a scoundrel who had a monetary interest in the local race track and published a newsletter of sorts with track results.

Originally working for none other than William Randolph

Hearst, Moses and his list of thugs cracked rival paper stand owners' skulls, burned their newsstands, and permanently disabled delivery cars. These were the results the Tribune wanted in order to secure its place in the newspaper business. When Marshall Field's stopped an ad in the Hearst Evening American, the Annenberg gang was sent to terrorize shoppers and employees by running up and down State Street shouting "Field's store closed." Marshall Field decided to run the ad.

Moses Annenberg eventually left the Hearst Empire and started his own wire service for what he called "upstanding citizens." His so-called worthy customers were men like Lucky Luciano and Meyer Lansky, who depended on current racetrack picks for bets. Moses, better known as Moe, with investment money from Al Capone and others, in 1929 founded the Nation-Wide News Service, which connected bookies and legitimate news organizations in two hundred cities to twenty-nine racetracks across the country. So the dollars began to flow. It wasn't long before the IRS began to smell a rat. In 1936, Moses Annenberg paid some $400,000 in back taxes.

If the circulation department issues weren't a big enough blemish for the Tribune, a boil was about to erupt. Labor was unhappy with current wages and benefits. The Tribune refused to offer more or even to listen to the complaints. The laborers, seeing no choice, threatened to strike. The newspaper couldn't afford the local competition to get the upper hand, so they called on Moe Annenberg for a solution to the problem. Moe suggested the newspaper hire Chicago's best labor consultant—Al Capone. In no time the terrorized workers were back on the job. Some workers returned with an arm in a sling, some with black eyes and badly bruised chins, and all of them with no raise. Capone's strong-armed ability to coerce didn't stop with the laborers. Capone's ability to convince judges and juries to rule in favor of the Tribune was seen time after time in court cases involving the Tribune. As Benny Binion stated many times, "He who has the gold makes the rules."

For the next several decades the Tribune ruled with an iron hand. The paper even hired the eminent Don Reuben to serve as the newspaper's attorney.

While Chicago dealt with its woes, Champaign was becoming more than a dot on the map. David Stevick, a Hungarian publisher from Hutchinson, Kansas, and owner of the Champaign Daily News, purchased the Champaign Daily Gazette in 1919, giving birth to the News-Gazette. At twenty-eight years old, he had demonstrated more editorial expertise than many publishers had in a lifetime career in the newspaper business. One of his editorial slogans was, "Be a booster and a builder." That he was. Very civic-minded, he promoted causes that would benefit the community, and he sharply criticized causes that were not in the public's best interest. Stevick's goal in publishing a rural community newspaper was to create a togetherness, or family, among the town folk and rural citizens. A shrewd business man, Stevick advanced his fortune shortly after WWI by buying land in the area that included railroad easements for the price of back taxes. Though noted for his head in business, Stevick had two vices: poker and alcohol. During one of the poker games, David, believing he had an unbeatable hand, bet everything he had, which included the News-Gazette. He lost. In due time David got the newspaper back in his name and swore off poker games.

The war ruined some and made others financially comfortable. With the funds acquired using property as collateral, Stevick purchased the Texarkana Gazette and the Texarkana News. He formed them into one paper, the Texarkana Gazette. He had 119 correspondents stationed all over Texas, Oklahoma, Louisiana, and Arkansas and subscribed to every known wire service. He also authored several books during this time, including: You and I with the Fleet, You and I in Hawaii, and You and I Tuna Fishing.

In August 1910, David married his sweetheart of several years, Helen Taylor. David bought an old Victorian home in

Texarkana and moved Helen into it shortly after the wedding. Not long after, on September 12, 1912, Helen gave birth to a daughter, Marajen.[4]

David referred to his new daughter as his cherub. When not at work, he doted on her and included her in everything he did.

Marajen's relationship with her father was close. She communicated with David better than with her mother. Helen Stevick, by far, preferred her professional life to raising a child. David taught Marajen hiking and other outdoor sports, which Marajen took to very quickly. An avid outdoorsman, David taught Marajen to appreciate nature and instilled in her the necessity of replacing trees and plants disturbed or uprooted for buildings. Together, father and daughter would roam lakes and pastures and hike trails so they could study the various species of grasses and trees native to Illinois. Thanks to David's teachings, this respect for nature stayed with Marajen throughout her life.

David's pastime was fishing with his English pit bull Buster. The news editor and dog went everywhere together. On one fishing trip Buster fell overboard and was injured beyond repair by the outboard motor. The death of Buster upset David so much Marajen thought she would remedy the situation. She had Buster's body taken to the local mortuary and requested that the director patch the dog up and preserve him. When that was done the mortician was to mount the dog on wheels so her father could pull him around. This way David would still have Buster with him wherever he went. When Helen heard what Marajen was up to she went to the funeral home. When she saw what was happening to the dog, she demanded that the mortician stop and bury him. He did so. Helen was furious with Marajen but left the discipline to David. When David was told what Marajen had intended to do to preserve Buster, he hugged his daughter for her thoughtfulness, even though the idea was a bit bizarre. No punishment was rendered.

The Stevick family struggled during the Depression and David, the gambler, felt they could withstand the dwindling economy. But when the circulation of his newspaper dropped and his stock market investments plunged, David and Helen lost the Texarkana News. It was hard for the family and especially Marajen, who was smothered in luxury. She now saw her popularity decline when the paper was sold, and her parents talked of leaving the only town she knew. David, already aware of the Champaign community, sold what bits of property he had left, and the family moved to Champaign, Illinois.

David presented the move to Illinois to Marajen as an adventure. Explaining that Champaign was a university town, he drew mental pictures so Marajen would look forward to her new home.

While the Stevicks were settling in their new home in Champaign, Chicago was receiving a newcomer as well, a newcomer who would, one day, enter the life of Marajen Stevick.

# A Gangster Is Born

A grade school dropout, Filippo Sacco craved the power and the pocket cash the neighborhood thugs flashed. Born in the tenements of Boston on June 4, 1905, to Italian immigrants, he learned the financial advantage of shakedowns and later the dirty art of murder on the streets. Not wanting to involve his family in his preferred life style, he dropped the family name on the streets and for public discussion around age sixteen. He engaged in petty thefts and vandalism and hung out with the thugs of Boston, dreaming of the day when they would include him in their circle. His father, a poor but honest businessman, threw him out of the home and told him never to come back. Sacco lived on the streets with his newfound friends, only keeping up with family news through his brother. He saw to it that his brother, sister, and mother had extra money from the thefts he committed, but he never returned to his home. Sacco may have been the black sheep of the family, but he never lost the bond he had with his siblings and especially his mother, Maria Sacco.

Wanting to stay in with the East Coast criminal underworld, Filippo became a fugitive of the law by the age of eighteen. Trafficking drugs had been a slick and profitable job for him. He was spotted by Federal agents peddling morphine to an addict by the name of Fisher. Both were arrested and put in jail. Maria could not make bail for Filippo, but someone in the crime world did. Fisher remained in the dingy, damp cell while Filippo was back on the streets. Needing a fix, Fisher knew a sure way to get out of jail. He contacted the Feds and agreed to sell out Filippo Sacco as his drug contact for a reduced sentence. Sacco put all the pieces together and, figuring Fisher to be the snitch, decided to settle the score.

On the day they both were to appear in court, Filippo Sacco showed up but Fisher didn't. In fact, no one had seen Fisher of late, nor would they ever again. Though no proof was found, it is believed that Filippo Sacco had everything to do with Fisher's disappearance. With no witness for the prosecution, the charges were dropped and Sacco walked. Uncomfortable that his name was becoming popular in police headquarters, Sacco skipped town to Chicago.

Already an apprentice in crime, Sacco was brought to the attention of a Chicago furniture salesman, Al Capone. Capone had been given the authority to run the 'Chicago Outfit' by John Torrie, who had been severely injured in an assassination attempt. Gang wars were going strong due to Prohibition. More gangsters had to be recruited if Capone was to increase his territory and power. To fit in with Capone's band of hoodlums, a gangster had to possess a lust for murder, which Sacco had no trouble proving he had. Pursuing the jobs Capone ordered from his gang won Sacco recognition from Al's lieutenants and an audience with Capone himself. This was the highest accolade a gangster could receive.

This was the one time that Filippo Sacco could have stopped and weighed his options. He could go back to the simple, respectable, honest life he was raised in or be accepted into the murky criminal underworld that required killing on order and all the illegal disciplines connected with it. Sacco had one choice, one he couldn't recant later and live! In the Capone headquarters at the Hawthorne Hotel in Chicago, Sacco chose the handshake and dinner Capone offered him. In doing so he accepted Capone's offer to join his family, the fraternity known as the Mafia.

The bullheaded, selfish, evil gang leader Capone found Sacco easy to like and had Filippo accompany him to several social gatherings. At the Hawthorne, Al convinced Sacco to change his name to one of "respectable Italian heritage." Dropping the name Filippo Sacco, he chose Rosselli.

Now a "made" Mafioso, in the early 1920s Rosselli craved the stacks of money he saw come in from bootleggers, loan sharks, bookmakers, and pimps. But he preferred to be soft-spoken and remain in the shadows. He wasn't leader material, and he knew it. "Let those that are loud and pushy and want in the spotlight be noticed. They will be the ones taking the heat. I'll be there to rake in the cash while they are let's say …out of town!" Johnny told a Vegas mobster.[5]

Johnny was well liked in Chicago and stayed in good graces with his boss. But there was a problem. Johnny had tuberculosis. Chicago could be damp and harsh like Boston. Lake Michigan brought icy, sharp winds that ripped through the city, causing every day to be a challenge for Johnny. Having done all they could medically, the doctors suggested a warmer climate if he wanted to live. Rosselli told Capone his dilemma, and Capone immediately made the necessary arrangements to get Rosselli out of Illinois and into California.

Rosselli wasn't immediately accepted by the tanned and ever-smiling hordes of wannabe movie stars. The main theme in Hollywood was the art of illusion. Don't appear to be who you really are, a philosophy that was right up Johnny's alley! Rosselli was enthralled by the film industry and actually found bit parts in the movies. Vivacity was a requirement, and Johnny was rich in that. He had the drive to be a movie star, and goodness knows he had the looks, but he didn't have the health. It took many, many months for his gaunt frame to fill out and his pale skin to tan.

Surviving in California wasn't easy in the beginning. Bit parts in movies didn't pay for the rent and luxuries too. He was reduced to freelancing for the wise guys for income. All he had known in his twenty-plus years was hoodlums becoming winners by force.

It was Rosselli's nature to choose plans and plots that reaped fast rewards, so he mingled in extortion, bribery, and narcotics. When highly connected criminals needed assistance, Johnny was their man. Because having morals was at the bottom of his list of virtues, Rosselli had no problem carrying a gun or using it. He may not have made a reputation in the film industry, but he sure did with the West Coast wise guys.

When Johnny wasn't doing odd jobs for crime figures, he worked on his language and demeanor. He studied the dress of people in power and learned the names of good wines. By the time Rosselli was in his thirties, he was remembered as being handsome and suave. He had forged a trusting relationship with studio dynasties and stars that made their careers in the studios, such as Jean Harlow, Jack Benny, and George Burns. Money from his "odd jobs" afforded him upscale lodging that brought him into contact with Ernest Hemingway, Greta Garbo, Humphrey Bogart, and others. He was well thought of and now had enormous influence among high-powered people. While Rosselli was making a name for himself in California, a little girl was growing up in Central Illinois who would one day turn his head.

# A Newspaper Heiress Grows Up

Marajen Stevick's artistic talent was recognized when she began painting at age eight. She developed her own style and preferred water colors to oils. The arts were in Marajen's blood, as it was with her maternal grandmother and aunts. Marie Stevick, Marajen's aunt, headed the art department at Skinners School of Music in Bloomington, Illinois, and was a noted landscapist. Marajen's mother, Helen, attended the same school and excelled in music. Marajen's academics didn't suffer either. While living with relatives in Arkansas for a few years she graduated from Texarkana Junior High on June 3, 1926. Her classmates remember her as a bratty kid with money. School chums remembered her for staging pranks during class time and pretending, to her girlfriends, she had aristocracy in her family. Most of her classmates didn't figure she would amount to anything.

The summer following her junior high graduation she moved back to Illinois. Four years later she began high school, and in 1930, at age fifteen, Marajen graduated from University High School in Urbana, Illinois. Marajen didn't take the question of whether to attend college seriously, though academically she would have done well. She found school work a bore and unchallenging, as well as the lack of social life that came with it. Her mother tried to persuade her to attend college. The University of Illinois was in their town, or Marajen could attend the college of her choice if she wanted to. Her father even assured her he could gain her admittance to Bryn Mawr or Mount Holyoke College, but Marajen wouldn't hear of it. She told her parents she had better things to do than sit in a classroom. Helen Stevick reminded her of the social life she could experience, but Marajen shot back with "Yes, and homework too!"

Classmate Bobbie Eisner, of the Eisner's Food Stores chain, remembered Marajen as "Very smart. Very outgoing and always looking for fun. School work seemed to come easy for her and she always had a busy social life!"[6]

Other friends said Marajen was like any teenage girl. She had utopian dreams of becoming a star. She craved the life of movie stars, specifically the life of Greta Garbo. Marajen would mimic Garbo's voice and mannerisms when called upon to recite in class. This frustrated her teachers, and Marajen often received a detention for her role playing. She liked dressing up in her mother's gowns, and she paraded around her home claiming she was a queen and ordered her parents around as if they were subservient to her. She loved shopping with her mother, Helen, but she had her mother's taste for only the best—often throwing tantrums to get what she wanted. She bought movie magazines and told her friends that some day she would be on the cover. She would tease her girlfriends, saying she was movie material and had the face for the silver screen. Marajen told high school classmates that she wanted to be a wife of luxury, and she would do what ever it took to be one. Her high school friends noted that Marajen was most often a sweet, likable person but could be devious and calculating about getting what she wanted.

In her late teens Marajen surprised no one that really knew her. She developed early physically, and she had attended enough adult functions that she could carry on an intelligent, witty conversation with most anyone. She had already developed a taste for the fast crowd and quickly became a femme fatale to the male gender. Tall, blond, and leggy, Marajen liked enticing the college boys by pulling risqué stunts at baseball or football practices at the university football stadium. She attended drinking parties with older friends, often ignoring the curfew David and Helen had set for her. Being the desirable date for fraternity brothers, Marajen exercised her "throw caution to the wind" attitude, which eventually caught up with her. The young man involved was a football star and had a brilliant future. His parents were furious and let him know that under no circumstances was he going to throw that future away. David Stevick came to the rescue by arranging a trip to Switzerland for Marajen. She would stay several weeks and then return home. When Marajen's absence was noticed, friends and relatives were told she had enrolled in a finishing school which, in a way, it was.

When Marajen returned to Illinois, David contacted relatives, who took Marajen on an extended trip to California for the purpose of further education. This didn't go as planned, as Marajen had other ideas. When not shopping at designer boutiques, she attended parties through invitations from people she hardly knew and whom her parents certainly wouldn't have approved of. At one social event Marajen met Charles Rogers, who was a B-movie actor in such films as Mexican Spitfire's Baby in 1941. On a whim, Marajen married his brother, B. H. Rogers. David, once again, rescued Marajen by having the marriage annulled. Furious at her father's intervention, Marajen turned around and married him again! It is believed that she suffered a miscarriage during this marriage. Once recovered, Marajen divorced B. H. Rogers and went back to Champaign.

When not dreaming of bright lights and movie roles, Marajen was learning the newspaper business from her father. She doted on David Stevick's every word and learned fast. David started training Marajen in the newspaper business from the stump up. She learned what wood was used, how the logs were prepared and turned into pulp, as well as the market for purchasing the pulp. At the newspaper she learned from reporters how they prepared their reports for print. Marajen studied under the general assignment team to see how assignments were distributed, to whom, and why. She also worked side by side with her mother, Helen, in learning the financial part of the newspaper business. David felt his daughter should be well-versed in the newspaper business, because his hope was that one day she would assume the responsibility for producing the newspaper, which often fell on Helen Stevick while David was off at business meetings or looking for other paper businesses to buy.

Helen had a good business head and dealt well with the white-collar sector of the paper. From her, Marajen learned the difference between white-collar and blue-collar employees. She made a promise to herself that although she might someday own a newspaper, she wouldn't make it her vocation in life.

David Stevick's last business trip involved wrapping up the business details of starting a radio station in Champaign. On December 15, 1935, David stopped for the night in Thomasville, Georgia. He had health problems for many years, and that night David William Stevick fell sick and died of a heart attack at age forty-eight. Helen and Marajen were devastated. Helen, who made her work the center of her universe, took David's death hard. She loved him and had worked side by side with him through the good years and bad. She had crafted the takeover of the Urbana Courier newspaper and worked with David on fine-tuning out of state deals. Now it was over.

Marajen grieved for her father. He was her mentor and best friend. This was the only time friends saw a reticent Marajen. She was uncommunicative for days. For over a week she withdrew from the paper and social events. She took no phone calls; nor did she read the telegrams of sympathy that came from all over the country. Marajen's doctor ordered complete bed rest for several days. Marajen cooperated.

Helen, wishing to carry out David's wish for the newspaper to remain locally owned and operated, stepped into the role of president and publisher of the News-Gazette. Maintaining the day-to-day operations, doing article checks, and attending reporter meetings made for eighteen-hour days. But Helen was determined to hang on to the business and succeed as a women publisher. With Marajen on the mend, the two of them sorted out the business affairs, keeping business investments that were profitable and selling those that did not produce the expected revenue. Most of the stock in various national papers was sold to maintain a healthy cash flow for the News-Gazette. Helen did keep, however, the stock in the Chicago Tribune.

Together, Helen and Marajen continued the radio station project, and on January 24, 1937, the radio station that bears David's initials, WDWS-AM, signed on the air. This was this huge plus for Champaign, as the St. Louis Cardinals baseball games were soon aired on the station.

Marajen, having learned all phases of the paper business from her parents, helped her mother by selling advertisements, reporting the club, church, and other social news, and working alongside her mother in the office. Her spunk came naturally, and though not enamored with all aspects of the newspaper, she proved to be a dexterous employee.

Helen Stevick was also known for her spontaneity and unpredictable behavior. She would often play gags at work, which frustrated Marajen to no end. Helen would hide articles that Marajen had been assigned at the News-Gazette on the morning the finished work was to go to press. Marajen would literally tear the office up looking for it. When Marajen's back was turned Helen would slip the paperwork onto Marajen's desk as if it had been there all the time. Tantrums from both women could be heard by employees when such so-called jokes were played. Though the two were not always compatible when deadlines were due mother and daughter got down to business.

Settling David Stevick's personal business and running the newspaper was exhausting work. Marajen often came in to work late and left early due to her assignments leaving the balance of daily responsibilities to her mother. With little time for mourning the death of David, Helen decided she and Marajen needed a vacation.

# Nightclubs, Movie Stars, and Mobsters

Early in 1936, Helen and Marajen chose sunny California for a breather from the newspaper business and the sudden death of David. California was a mysterious place to be in the 1930s. It was the home of movie stars that Marajen dreamed of equaling. Even though many of the stars and producers had been black listed, Marajen saw herself rubbing elbows with the people who made Hollywood the glamorous zone. She also knew that art galleries lined the sidewalks. Marajen made the art gallery circuit, where she held lengthy conversations with brilliant and talented artists about paintings by Matisse, Renoir, and Picasso. Movie stars in the '30s never lost their sparkle. Stars like Myrna Loy captivated Marajen; both women were stylish, classy, and witty. Marajen scanned the movie tabloids to find where the stars ate, shopped, and relaxed.

When it came to dining, both Helen and Marajen wanted to be with the movie stars. The Musso and Frank Grill on Hollywood Boulevard was a hot spot in Tinsel Town. Helen bragged when she returned to Champaign that William Faulkner had held the door for her and Marajen to enter the popular restaurant. To miss Sunset Boulevard, on this trip, would have been a sin. Helen made an appointment with Billy Wilkerson, owner of the Hollywood Reporter, for the sole purpose of introducing herself and Marajen. It just didn't hurt to drop names and bank accounts in this town! That evening Wilkerson treated Marajen and Helen to dinner at the Mocambo nightclub. A dress code was strictly enforced at the club, allowing Marajen to dress lavishly, meet important people, and, most of all, photographed. This was the club that guaranteed sightings of starlets and those aspiring to be somebody. Finally, Marajen was in her element.

Rodeo Drive, the upscale shopping street, was high on the vacation agenda. But the Stevicks couldn't just take a taxi. Helen hired a Rolls Royce and a driver to escort them on their shopping spree. Helen, known for her impulsive buying, could now afford this habit without the usual friction when David received the bills. Marajen quickly picked up the taste for expensive things; for the first time she could buy what she wanted and as much as she wanted. Shoes, dresses, perfumes, and jewelry topped the list of what Marajen deemed necessities. Boutique shops for the upscale chic shopper were like a dream come true for Marajen. The famed shopping sites allowed Marajen to charge using only her signature. The bills would later be paid by the newspaper. Both women enjoyed dining at expensive restaurants and vintage wines. Helen wasted no time letting people know who she was and that money was not a concern. Marajen took mental notes about how her mother was accepted in exclusive places and stored them for future use.

By 1937 Johnny Rosselli was connected enough that he could give up his simple duplex and take up residency in a luxurious apartment just blocks from Beverly Hills. He was chauffeured to "business meetings" and regularly had lunch at the Brown Derby. He became friends with starlets such as the Gabor Sisters and a rising young star by the name of June Lang. One day while table hopping and chatting with Vincent Barbi, a prize fighter, he spotted a young, statuesque lady in a yellow sundress sitting at a table with other women. Rosselli walked over and, looking straight into Marajen's eyes, said, "People call me Johnny. May I ask what your name is?" To that the young lady smiled and said, "Marajen Stevick." The other women at the table recognized him and asked Johnny to sit with them. After their luncheon Rosselli asked Marajen if she had ever seen a horse race. When she said no, he invited her and Helen to join him at the Santa Anita racetrack.

Once they were settled in box seats at the track, Rosselli excused himself for an unexpected meeting and returned when the last race was almost over. Johnny's meeting probably was to check on the Mob's interest in the wire service betting business at the race track. Seeking forgiveness for being rude, Johnny asked Marajen to dinner that night. Marajen, already infatuated with the macho Johnny, eagerly accepted. Over dinner that night, Marajen and Johnny talked about show business, and Marajen expressed her love for movie stars and the rich and famous. It is not known if Marjen thought that Rosselli could help her meet movie producers and possibly land a bit part or simply rub elbows with them.

Over the next few years Johnny and Marajen shared several weekday lunches at various hot spots in Hollywood when she and Helen visited friends. One late afternoon, Johnny and Marajen entered the Trocadero Club, a popular hangout for movie producers, stars, and gangsters. Entering the Trocodero Club, the crown jewel of the Sunset Strip nightspots, Marajen and Johnny were greeting by a scantily dressed coat-check girl who ushered them into the cream and gold entrance area of the dinning room. The rapscallion Johnny led Marajen up to the copper-topped bar, where he introduced her to movie producer Harry Cohn and actress Joan Crawford. Earlier, Rosselli had been told by Chicago boss Tony Accardo to convince Cohn to sign on an unknown movie actress by the name of Marilyn Monroe. Harry didn't want to take on an unsure investment, but he agreed to do so because he had purchased Columbia

Pictures with Mob money. And a personal threat was made on Cohn if he didn't.

While the group stood at the bar, Cohn, very intoxicated, made an off-colored remark to Marajen. Quick-witted Marajen made one back, which caused Cohn's cohorts to immediately put their drinks on the bar and take a step back. Cohn, known for his vulgar mouth and quick temper, looked to Marajen and then to Johnny and burst out laughing. Looking at Rosselli, Cohn said, "I like this broad! Let me buy her a drink!" Johnny casually made an excuse to Cohn, and he and Marajen left. Johnny knew he had to be careful around Cohn due to Cohn's influence with the West Coast Mob family, and he wasn't ready to let Marajen in on his true occupation. Marajen, on the other hand, was disappointed at not being able to speak with Miss Crawford or settle the score with Cohn. She stated to friends that Joan Crawford was absolutely beautiful and that Harry Cohn wasn't the god he had been made out to be.[7]

Although her stay in California was somewhat brief Johnny and Marajen managed to attend two parties at the Brown Derby, where Marajen met Lana Turner and Donna Reed. She also met Joe Schenck, another movie production company owner. Young, impressionable Marajen, putting two and two together, thought being seen socially with Johnny could mean being a headliner in a movie someday. But the favorite was the Trocadero Club which catered to celebrities, moneymakers, and gangsters. Decorated in silver and glass, the club was the show room for up and coming artists who wanted their crafts viewed by those who were willing to pay the asking price. Johnny was well-known by most of the luscious topless beauties that made up the chorus line and the managers. Though Marajen was Johnny's date, he would be called away to attend to some "business" that needed his attention. Clubs such as the Trocadero were often just storefronts to conceal illegal gambling and the laundering of dirty money, leaving its legacy stained in blood. Marjen always accepted Johnny's excuses for his lengthy departures and waited patiently for his return. A few years later the Trocadero Club was sold to Bugsy Siegel and Mickey Cohn, under pressure from the gangsters.

At Marajen's request, Johnny took her to the famous Brown Derby, which was Loretta Young's favorite hangout. The black-tie restaurant always had a camera girl in its employ, and Marajen liked nothing better than to be photographed and written about in the Hollywood Reporter. If Marajen could accomplish being photographed followed by a write-up she would make the section of who's who in Hollywood. It would be a dream come true for her.

Though Rosselli enjoyed Marajen's company, he was far too busy to enjoy the charms of this dreamy-eyed maiden for long. After a week long hiatus with Marajen he graciously bowed out of her life …for a while.

There was work to be done at home, so Helen and Marajen left California and returned to Champaign, much to Marajen's dismay. Helen needed to finish other projects that David Stevick had begun. Now that WDWS-AM radio was on the air, there were advertisements to secure and other day-to-day radio business. WDWS was Champaign County's first commercial radio station, and Helen didn't want it to fail. Neighboring stations had been all but ignored in advertisements by the News-Gazette. The News-Gazette was strict about not printing news information from competing media. Programs for WDWS-AM were broadcast from the second floor of the original News-Gazette. The call letters for the radio station bore David Stevick's initials was the decision made by Helen and Marajen. Shortly, the sister station, WHMS-AM, joined the family, which became the flagship station for the University of Illinois. About ten years later WDWS-FM went on the air, bringing the first commercial FM signal to East Central Illinois.

Marajen seemed satisfied with the presence of local guests who were interviewed at the stations, but no one met her criteria for a suitable mate. She was always on the hunt for a husband, a desire shared by her mother. Marajen had loved the affluent, extravagant lifestyle of California and was enamored with Johnny Rosselli. After a few months at home she convinced her mother to let her return to the West Coast alone. Marajen wanted more excitement in her life than doing the social club circle for a local newspaper and scheduling people for interviews at the radio stations. She wanted lights, music, and romance. She wanted to taste the fabulous lifestyle she had been introduced to in the make-believe world of Hollywood, and she wanted to see Johnny.

Marajen's ambition plus Johnny's shrewd, cunning ways made them an interesting couple. Once again on the nightclub circuit, Marajen delved into renewing acquaintances with bright, lovely stars and affluent people like Lorretta Young, Jack Warner, Walter Annenberg, and Charles Lucky Luciano. Johnny, on the other hand, was being Johnny!

While no written proof is known to exist, Marajen's friends say that Johnny and Marajen were married during this trip. Marajen, raised in a deeply religious home and fearing her mother's wrath if the tabloids leaked her affair with Johnny Rosselli, found a moral way around it. Marajen and Johnny would marry under assumed names. The wedding ceremony was short and simple. No photos, per the order of Johnny, and no parties afterward, which didn't please Marajen at all. She had purchased a gorgeous white satin and lace floor-length gown that emphasized her hourglass figure. The long sleeves were gathered at her wrists with rolled satin. The gown was designed by Howard Greer, who told Marajen that her dress was the best he had yet designed. Marajen had expected Johnny to throw a wedding party for them, but instead there was nothing. The honeymoon never left the hotel suite and it, too, was short and sweet. But marriage didn't change Johnny, and his roving eye captured another beautiful woman he knew from years back, June Lang.

The marriage between Marajen Stevick and Johnny Rosselli, not made in heaven, was annulled and wiped from the records a few weeks later by a "connected" judge. Marajen complained to her California friends that Johnny wouldn't take her anywhere or introduce her to anyone important. The naive young woman could only see the glamorous side of Johnny, not the business side that required a low profile and sudden disappearances for days at a time. Johnny, on the other hand, made no excuses. "She was just a broad ...a pretty one, but a broad," Rosselli told his bookie.[8]

Marajen wasted no time showing Rosselli she could get anyone she chose, and days after the annulled marriage she was seen being seated at a table next to Lucky Luciano at the Star Dust casino. Marajen and Lucky conversed, and Lucky bought a few rounds of drinks. Also sitting around the table were Judy Garland, jazz clarinetist Artie Shaw, and the Gabor sisters.[9] Hoping the night club gossip would get back to Johnny, Marajen savored her evening with Lucky and returned home to Illinois a few days later.[10]

It was just as well that her marriage to Johnny ended when it did. While Marajen was safe in Champaign helping to run the News-Gazette newspaper, the Justice Department was taking a very close look at Johnny Rosselli. His old buddy, Joe Schenck of the film studios, was being indicted on tax violations and conspiracy charges stemming from a $100,000 loan to Willie Bioff, a low-level gangster and pimp. Bioff and Rosselli had cooked up a scheme to shake down thousands from the film industry. It probably would have gone unnoticed for a long time had not Bioff started skimming thousands for himself from the motion picture studios. Bioff was charged with labor racketeering and tax evasion. Knowing the Feds had the goods on him, Bioff worked out a deal. Testifying against his friends, including Rosselli, Bioff received a reduced sentence.

Once Bioff was sentenced and began his life within prison walls, he soon learned prison was not for him. He let his colleagues know, from his prison cell, that he wanted out of the Mob. The very next day Louis Campagna, a ruthless Capone hit man, visited Willie Bioff and asked him if he really wanted out. He nodded. Louis told him that he could indeed resign from the Family, but it would be feet first and in a brand new pair of cement shoes. Knowing exactly what that meant, Bioff changed his mind.

Rosselli didn't fare much better. A subpoena was served on Rosselli to testify in Bioff's trial, and now Rosselli was known to the Feds in California. This was publicity Rosselli didn't need. He escaped going to prison but should have been found guilty of perjury. His marriage to actress June Lang in 1940 was drawing to a close, again due to his romantic interest in another actress, Helen Greco. The federal investigators pushed Johnny into joining the army. But the army didn't hide Rosselli for long. In March of 1943 Johnny was arrested on racketeering charges and sentenced to ten years. He was paroled in 1946 after serving only three years. Once free, Johnny went back to California but kept a low profile. He made no contact with Marajen after his release.[11]

Helen, believing she needed to keep Marajen on a short leash, decided to make her co-publisher of the News-Gazette. This pleased Marajen and she took an active interest in the operation and decision making for the paper. She did well at it, too, even though she and her mother would butt heads at times, which led to loud, angry arguments and more tantrums, both at the paper and home.

Because her job was now more demanding and stressful, Marajen spent many Saturday nights at Chanute Air Force Base in Rantoul, Illinois, as a means of escape. The large training air base in the heart of Illinois was only a few minutes from Champaign. There, Marajen enjoyed the attention the fly-boys bestowed upon her. Drinking and dancing to bands and listening to the latest war stories interested Marajen. At Chanute, Marajen could forget who she was and just be a young woman. She dated some of the officers and even introduced a couple to her mother.[12] But Marajen didn't stay satisfied for long. Her restless nature and need for attention and the spot light sent her back to California to meet up with friends who could bring her up to date on Johnny.

Learning that Johnny Rosselli had married June Lang infuriated Marajen, but she found it humorous that June had divorced him and that Johnny had joined the army. Marajen mused that Johnny was probably sorry he had left her. Feeling competition from starlets in California in her pursuit of capturing a wealthy husband, Marajen made several comments at a night club that she could get anybody she wanted …just like Johnny.

Helen, trying to keep Marajen in the neighborhood, sent her to Chicago to further her knowledge of the newspaper business through intense training at the Tribune. In Chicago, Marajen spent her days working with employees of the Chicago Tribune, which she found harder than work at the News-Gazette in Champaign. She did enjoy working with the street reporters, who were known for their crime scene reporting at all hours of the night. Marajen found this exciting but mainly far too gory for her. She maintained that she couldn't wear her fancy clothes and rarely were important people involved. Marajen spent her free time socializing in Chicago's nightlife. Through Tribune associates, she met Ralph Jones, a special agent for the Continental Causality Company. True to nature, Marajen married Ralph and divorced him shortly afterwards. Though Jones was financially comfortable, he did not meet Marajen's criteria for wealth or social prominence.

Marajen's social life could have tarnished her reputation, but she had a solution for that issue. Marajen joked to her friends in California that she had never slept with anyone that she wasn't married to.

A few months after her divorce from Ralph Jones, Marajen began displaying abnormal conduct. She became quite irresponsible with money and her mannerisms. She bought extravagant gifts for people she didn't know well and caused ugly scenes in restaurants in Chicago. Her spending in upscale stores drew the attention of shop owners, who contacted Helen. Minutes afterwards Marajen would have no recollection of her actions. She would swear to her mother that the store managers didn't know what they were talking about or that they had confused her with someone else.

Over a period of time Helen stepped in and inquired about medical treatment for Marajen. Learning the facts from doctors Helen requested shock treatments for Marajen. This medical treatment was quite common at that time for cases of depression or abnormalities in the brain. Where and when this was done is unknown but it's believed not to have happened in Illinois. Once on the mend, Marajen recuperated in San Francisco and became a semi-regular at Lefty O'Doul's restaurant.

Marajen never relented in her quest for fame and kept herself surrounded by notorious people. She still craved the attention of the rich and famous. She still dreamed of her name in lights. She demanded to be the center of attention, and she was determined to get attention no matter what the cost. Marajen just couldn't see she already had both fame and wealth as a birthright.[13]

Recuperating from another divorce, Marajen satisfied her craving for the limelight by taking in parties in Hollywood after a few weeks of rest. On this trip to Tinsel Town she met Debbie Reynolds and accepted invitations to parties that Debbie and her husband hosted. Debbie found Marajen a delight to know and enjoyed her unconventional wit. Marajen also became close to Loretta Young. This encounter between Marajen and Loretta set the stage for an enduring relationship that lasted for years. When not working on a movie or her weekly television show, Loretta visited Marajen in Champaign. When not having parties at her Champaign home where she would introduce Loretta to friends and business associates,

Marajen would charter a jet and fly to New York or Miami to shop and socialize with the rich and famous there. The friendship ended abruptly on one visit, when Marajen greeted Loretta at the door and promptly told Loretta that she would have to sleep in the maid's quarters instead of the main house. Loretta, feeling humiliated, returned home the same day.

Helen, noting some changes in Marajen's personality, consulted the doctor who had performed previous shock treatments about the possibility that the personality and mental changes Marajen had previously experienced could return. The doctor had no conclusive insights.

Undaunted by her attitude toward Loretta Young, when in California Marajen continued to work her social circle. She dined with film producers and movie studio heads, always looking for the wealthy, prominent man that she hoped would take her for a wife. The statuesque beauty could be seen any evening on the arm of a movie mogul or film producer, often causing a scene in the nightclub should a wife also be present. When this happened, Marajen would fly home to avoid tabloid scandal.

Home in Champaign, Helen was busy with the paper and expressed her need for Marajen to be around more. Marajen cooperated and fine-tuned her business skills. But the class of people she wanted around her was not in Champaign, so she brought her California friends to Illinois. Not finding adequate entertainment for her guests in Champaign, Marajen would charter a plane to take her and her California friends to Mexico or some Caribbean island. Her thirst for attention and dominance seemed never to be satisfied. Parties in the Caribbean were usually held in lavish hotels, where Marajen would have a well-known dress designer make her gowns that were worn only once and then stored away. Her guest lists would include politicians, high-ranking military personnel, and movie stars, if they were on the island. Her parties would often last two full days, at the cost of thousands of dollars.

# Future War Hero
# Marries Marajen

World War II captivated everyone's attention. Food was expensive, factories were being converted into munitions plants, and young men dropped out of college and answered the boldly colored posters that hung everywhere, saying Uncle Sam Wants You! The United States, expecting Japan to attack the Philippines and not Pearl Harbor, wasn't totally ready. The Air Force, in particular, with its outdated somewhat obsolete equipment, wasn't war-ready. But they were about to get an outstanding pilot.

Twenty-six-year old Captain Ed Dyess stood over six feet and was slender, with the Texan drawl and charisma. The son of Judge Dyess and Hallie Graham Dyess, Edwin was raised in a typical cow town, where men wore ten-gallon hats and spurs that jingled when they walked. Albany, Texas, was the county seat of Shackelford County. Ranching and cow punching were the main occupations when Edwin was a boy. On Main Street in Albany stands a bronze tablet topped with a steer's head memorializing the 1875 to 1890 Texas Cattle Trail to Dodge City. Farther down the street another statue stands, commemorating the first oil well to strike in 1919.

Judge and Mrs. Dyess were hoping to have their son excel in school and maybe become a teacher. Edwin's father had steadily moved up in politics and thought his son would follow in those footsteps. But Edwin had other ideas. His grades fell, and he was cited for having a bad attitude in the class room; Edwin's elementary teachers contacted his parents. When Judge Dyess expressed his concern over the poor grades to his son, Edwin told his father not to worry; he wouldn't need an education, as he was going to join the carnival,

Graduating from secondary school and childish dreams, Edwin attended John Tarleton College at Stephenville, Texas. His goal was to be an attorney. Another dream entered Edwin's head about this time. He had been thrilled with Lindberg's flight in 1927 from New York to Paris. With much thought, he announced to his parents that he had decided to be an aviator.

After graduation from Kelly Ffield as second lieutenant, Edwin Dyess transferred to Shreveport, Louisiana. His second transfer was to Hamilton Field in California, where he was promoted to first lieutenant and at the same time given command of the 21st Pursuit Squadron.

Accepting a dinner party invitation at the home of friends in San Francisco, Edwin met his future bride. Marajen Stevick was there visiting friends of her parents. The relationship blossomed quickly, and they were married in the early spring of 1941. A few days after a short honeymoon, Dyess reported back to his squadron to prepare to sail to Manila. In May of 1941, Dyess made a quick trip to Champaign, Illinois, to see Marajen one more time. When Edwin Dyess left Champaign, he was leaving the closest thing to heaven and about to enter pure hell. The new Mrs. Dyess would not hear from her husband until a telegram arrived in Champaign stating that he was a prisoner of war.

An expert pilot, Dyess completed mission after mission after the bombing of Pearl Harbor, and he assisted his comrades when he saw they were in trouble. In late February, Dyess had been summoned to headquarters and told by his chief air officer that the 21$^{st}$ was all but a suicide squadron. This bore heavily on Dyess, and he hoped his men, as young as they were, were ready for what lay ahead. He continued to boost morale when some were ready to give up. They had been hit hard by the Japanese and suffered the loss of many planes. Then, as the Japanese army attacked again, more planes and many more men were lost. When they had hardly anything left, Dyess gathered about 110 of his men and officers of the 21$^{st}$ Pursuit with the intent of reaching Corregidor, a good three-hour swim by water. There, the 21$^{st}$ could join General King and regroup. But this wasn't to happen.

Dyess's squadron learned that General King had surrendered to the Imperial Japanese army. In essence they were prisoners. On April 10, 1942, the prisoners began what was later called the Bataan Death March. The eighty-five-mile trip began on the outskirts of the province of Bataan en route to Pampanga exactly one day after his squadron surrendered. Sickened and weak, the American and Filipino soldiers fought to stay in marching formation under the tropical sun. Japanese soldiers would lean from their trucks to bash the heads of the staggering prisoners. Japanese soldiers pushed American soldiers to the ground, knowing they were too weak to move faster than the Japanese supply truck that would run over them. Forced to sit in the direct sunlight, prisoners would, after many hours of this torture, succumb to delirium and finally death. Some months later, Dyess sent a memo to Marajen stating he was in Philippine Military Prison Camp No. 2, that his health was good and he was receiving treatment. He requested that she keep her chin up and to tell family members not to worry and to bid them hello from him. Marajen was comforted by the fact that he was being treated well, or so she believed. She spoke of Edwin's condition to employees at the News-Gazette with confidence.

Of course this wasn't how it was for Dyess or the rest of

the prisoners. In the Japanese prison camps, all illnesses and ailments were left to run their course, which usually meant a nameless grave.

Dyess and a few of his men worked on the rice patty crew. He was not allowed to wrap his feet and legs to prevent getting cut and bruised. Soon his legs were covered with ulcers. A cut finger became infected to the point that he thought it would have to be amputated. Because of a diet of only rice, he became sick with scurvy, which left the inside of his mouth so raw that the only way to swallow was to throw his head back enough times, that the food fell down his throat.

Colonel Edwin Dyess and two others from his command survived the eighty-five-mile death march and, through cunning and the determination to live, eventually escaped through cunning and the determination to live. But six thousand soldiers didn't. After being rescued by an American submarine, Dyess recuperated from his war injuries in California and again took to the air five months after his Bataan ordeal. But tragedy was still looming over him. Ordered to report for duty with the 4th Air Force, Colonel Edwin Dyess was practicing flight patterns when his plane developed mechanical problems. To avoid crashing over a heavily populated area of Burbank, California, he flew his plane into mountains and was killed on December 22, 1943. He died a war hero, and Marajen Stevick Dyess was a widow. Marajen had visited Edwin while he was in the hospital and looked forward to him coming home when fully healed. She was shocked and despondent over the news of his crash. She had so little of Edwin left, only his memory, pictures, and the medals he had earned: the Silver Star, Legion of Merit, and the Distinguished Service Cross with one oak leaf cluster.

Edwin Dyess had written his memories of the Bataan Death March during his recuperation period and presented his account to the government. But the government didn't want the public to know of the horrible conditions he and other military personnel had been exposed to at the hands of the

Japanese army, so the report stayed in a desk drawer for months. In 1944, the Chicago Tribune published the Dyess memoirs, which drew furor from the American public over the treatment of our military personnel.[14]

While Marajen mourned the death of her husband, Helen was busy orchestrating a proposal to build an airport for the University of Illinois. University president Arthur Willard asked the board of trustees to aggressively pursue this plan. August C. Meyer, a local attorney, and Helen Stevick spoke with Illinois senators and other federal politicians to get action behind the plan. The cost would be $2,250,000; the proposed airport would sit on 762 acres southwest of Champaign. The University's share would be $750,000, and the rest of the funding would come from the State of Illinois funds. Construction began in May 1944. The completion of Willard Airport made major headlines. At its completion, it was the largest university airport in the world.

Work and no play was not Helen's style. She had lived the single life long enough and wished for a second husband. Credentials had to come with the husband, of course—wealth, position, power. Somewhere in her travels, Helen met a man who claimed to be a Spanish prince. Records indicate that he was a suave, conceited con-artist. Unfortunately Helen fell for him.

The courtship had been short when the prince proposed to Helen in the mid-40s. The almost-broke Helen accepted his proposal, believing he would be able to financially support her. The prince claimed that his funds were tied up in overseas accounts, so Helen agreed to fund the wedding, assuming the money would be transferred back afterwards. The Drake Hotel in Chicago was chosen to host the event. The wedding invitation list was to include only close friends and any dignitaries that Helen felt would give substantial monetary gifts. The menu for the reception was to include fresh chickens from the Champaign area prepared by the chefs at the Drake.

A banquet room was lavishly decorated. Helen and the "prince" had planned a winter wedding, which for most of Illinois meant freezing temperatures mixed with snow and ice. The chickens were to be transported from Champaign in a borrowed pickup truck to the Drake Hotel. Again, things didn't go as planned. By mid-day the weather turned for the worse. Temperatures in the teens and cold blowing winds caused most of the chickens to freeze to death during the trip. The chefs threw fits, but with the promise of additional pay they managed a last-minute change in the main course.

The ceremony was brief. After Helen and the prince mingled with all the guests, they retired to the honeymoon suite. Marajen, always one for grabbing the center of attention, decided to break the romantic spell on the wedding night. Climbing out of the window of her suite, she walked along the balcony edge to the newlyweds' suite. She climbed into the window of the new bride and groom's bedroom just as the marriage was being consummated and jumped into their bed. The shocked prince jumped out of the bed, grabbed his clothes, and left in a haze of vile language. The marriage was annulled shortly after.[15] Again, Marajen had taken center stage.

# I Michael, Take Thee, Marajen

It is unclear where Marajen Stevick Dyess met Michael Chinigo. Friends in Italy say Helen and Marajen were traveling in Italy with friends from California in the late 1940s so Marajen could visit a newspaper publisher in Rome. The intent was for Marajen to acquire international experience writing articles. Michael Chinigo, a man of notoriety as a journalist for the Italian News Service, just happened to be at the publishers the same day. He was introduced to Marajen by the newspaper staff. As usual, Marajen was found attractive by the journalist, so while Helen dealt with the newspaper business Michael and Marajen toured Rome.

Michael, born of Albanian royalty in August 1908, inherited the title of count at birth. His family history can be traced to the 1500s, when a monastery and some of the land around it was bequeathed to an Albanian exile group of about twenty families in exchange for annual payments in the form of livestock that was raised on the grounds. The Chinigo family was one of the twenty families to be granted this opportunity. Michael's family remained farmers until his paternal grandfather's royal blood line was recognized.

In 1915, Michael's mother brought her children to America, settling in Connecticut. Michael gained his U.S. citizenship and studied in both Rome and at Yale University. His course of studies was journalism, though his intention was to enter the medical profession. During his time in the United States Michael mastered seven languages. The outbreak of war stalled Michael's studies. With WWII raging, Michael, if nothing else, was torn between his birth country, Italy, and his adopted country, the United States. The Nazi-Fascist force in Italy was under attack by the underground forces of the OSS. Michael, returning to Rome to take up his medical studies, took employment, instead, as a reporter for the International News Service (INS). Sometime later Michael Chinigo would be recruited for the clandestine services for the OSS and would return to Sicily to participate in the campaign under the assumption he was covering the war campaign as a reporter. At this time, Michael was given the code name Sorel. In five weeks his group of secret investigators had fulfilled their assigned duties of transmitting strategic intelligence on the war. Michael proved to be a great asset to the United States in journalism. He had the ability to speak many Italian dialects and seemed able to befriend anybody. During his time in Sicily Michael was wounded in his arm and wrist and later received a Silver Star.

While his successes were many, so were the problems. The two governments still needed someone to use for advance work in Sicily. The U.S. Navel Intelligence persuaded the U.S. government to release Mafia kingpin Lucky Luciano from prison for this purpose. Lucky was to make the arrangements for the Sicily invasion of 1943. Michael Chinigo, working with Luciano, handled the minor work and details for the invasion. In the late 1940s the American CIA enlisted Michael to enter the world of spooks in a clandestine project. But training would precede actual work in this project and, oh yes, marriage.

If Marajen knew of Michael's underground activities with the government during the war, she never spoke of them to anyone. She certainly never mentioned her relationship with

Lucky Luciano to Michael. What interested her was the fact that Michael was a titled count.

Marajen fell in love with Italy. She loved touring ancient Rome's hidden streets and tracking the old haunted realm of deities hidden in the Eternal City. The museums of ancient statues sparked her interest in art, and the cobblestone walkways made her appreciate indulging in foaming cups of cappuccino. She learned specific Italian words and phrases that allowed her to roam the streets and communities with ease. She and Michael experienced it all when she flew in from the States with Helen's blessings. Marajen spent days in Naples, which she found an experience. Marajen would use her afternoons to kick the sand along the beaches and look for ancient vases with wine still in them from the early 1600s, as local legends told. She shopped in the out-of-the-way boutiques and chatted with the intellectually and culturally savvy clientele who were notorious for gathering in the back alley wineries and pastry shops. Afterwards she would take the cobblestone walkways out of town and climb the rugged terrain to watch the crashing waves of the Tyrrhenian Sea splatter on the sides of raised vineyards. Perching her easel on the rocks, she would spend the day capturing nature's moods on the canvas. She wrote her mother, telling of the beautiful colors of the waters and the architectural designs of the buildings. She utilized her talents by setting up an easel and painting some of the breathtaking views.

Marajen also found the Italians to be warm and receptive, even though they found her Italian dialect amusing. One food that Michael insisted upon was pizza made with tomatoes that had been grown in the rich volcanic soil of Vesuvius. Michael also showed her Italy via a sailing vessel many times. On one of the trips they sailed to shore to view an old twelfth-century monastery. Michael told Marajen he had visited the monastery as a child. This probably wasn't true because Michael's childhood was spent primarily in the States, but the story impressed

Marajen. The name of the old monastery was Torre di Civita in Ravello, Italy, and consisted of about 140 acres. The monastery, at one time, had been owned by Prince Luigi of Campamia, who was in King Vittorio Emanuel's court. Much later the villa was owned by a principessa, who died in 1945. She willed the villa to a German nobleman. Though it appeared to be quite beautiful, none of the former owners had taken proper care of it. Marajen, enamored of the relic, wrote her mother describing the monastery as being in horrible disarray but said she had to have it. She told Helen what renovations would do for the place and how she could make it "eye-catching beautiful." The young woman, infatuated with the count, expressed her true feelings for him to Helen. "Oh, Mother. He's a count! Can you believe it? I've met a real-life count!"

Around 1952 Marajen brought Helen to Italy to be introduced to Michael. Helen was impressed with the dashing, soft-spoken man whom Marajen had fallen in love with. With Helen's approval, Michael proposed to Marajen. On a weekend outing, Helen saw the monastery and agreed to buy it for them as a wedding gift. Marajen was ecstatic and immediately started drawing up plans to redo "her villa," as she called it.

Marajen contracted the master tradesmen in Italy for the repairs and additions to the villa. She worked with them on the design and the use of native materials for both the main house and the various gardens that were planted around the villa. When the restorations were completed, Michael and Marajen were married in a small ceremony in Rome in May 1953. Michael's earlier marriage to a Romanian opera singer had not been formally terminated when his marriage to Marajen occurred. Marajen was unaware of Michael's pending divorce, as Michael had never told Marajen about his other marriage.

The new Mrs. Chinigo and Helen returned to Champaign after the couple enjoyed a brief honeymoon, while Michael, working as a correspondent for the Randolph Hearst Corporation in Rome, stayed behind finishing a project. With this marriage to Count Michael Chinigo, Marajen had one of her dreams finally come true. She was titled …a countess. Over the next couple of years Helen visited the newlyweds in Italy several times. Mother and daughter became well acquainted with Italy through numerous tours throughout the country.

Back in America, the country was coming out of the war quite gracefully. Business was kicking into fourth gear. The population was booming, and life, overall, was good again. Hollywood was turning out movies and starlets right and left. Marilyn Monroe, who had already starred in a few B movies, was now being pushed to the front headlines of the movie scene.

Johnny Rosselli stated to the FBI that he was employed as a movie producer at Monogram Studios. Knowing the film producers well, Rosselli tried to impress the FBI with his now-legal career by saying he had a part in making Monroe a new star. In reality Rosselli was diverting his attention from the movies to the gambling mecca, Las Vegas. In the early '50s Rosselli, still considered a top hoodlum by the FBI, was the Los Angeles Mob's chief representative in Vegas. His job was to make sure both the Chicago and LA crime families got their share of the casino revenues. What he didn't tell the Feds about was his interest in a tiny country south of the United States.[16]

At the same time, Communism was becoming a household word in America. The news media carried accounts of a political revolution about to erupt in Cuba. The provocative Latin rhythm that rang throughout Cuba's nightclubs masked what was really going on in the country that lay just ninety miles off the coast of Florida. While the political revolution made the headlines, another deadly war was fermenting.

Cocaine and heroin, the drugs of choice, were being shipped out of Cuba by the Mob. The man behind the scenes of this industry was Florida's godfather; Santo Trafficante Jr. Trafficante openly operated the Sans Souci casino and held interests in the Tropicana and the Riviera casinos in Cuba.

He referred to his hotel operations as "constitutional" business holdings.

Santo Trafficante Jr. began his climb to power in southern Florida in the early 1950s. He had been schooled by the mobsters in New York at his father's request. He had a pleasant personality and was admired by the public. Little did the public know of Santo's use of brutal force to achieve what he wanted. In 1954, Santo's father died, and the position of Florida Mob boss was passed to Santo Jr. He maintained ties with the Bonanno crime family in New York City but was tightly connected to Sam Giancana of the Chicago Mob family.

Batista, then ruler of Cuba, wanted a larger share of the drug money and the gambling rackets run by the Mob in Cuba. The Mob, holding the reins in Cuba, made Havana the playground of the rich and famous because of the high-roller money that poured into the Mob's purse. While the Mob maintained focus on the casino and drug businesses, a man with a small following continued to plan a revolution within the island of Cuba. Fidel Castro and his revolutionaries wanted to overtake the Fulgencio Batista dictatorship through the implementation of new social and economic programs. The Cuban people were ready for this change and joined in. Batista's military forces far outnumbered Castro's but were overthrown in 1959. Mob figures looked at the political revolution as having a positive effect on their business. Cuba's new ruler Fidel Castro wouldn't care that much about the Mob's holdings—or would he?

Late in 1959, Santo Trafficante Jr. went to Cuba to ensure the Mob's position with casinos. Until 1959, according to the books, the Tropicana was barely breaking even by serving drinks and meals. The profit from gambling was bringing in around $5,000 a day, after the Mob took their percentage. A man whom Marajen had met in Hollywood kept himself in the shadows of the Cuban drug business.

His training under the CIA leadership now finished, Michael Chinigo concentrated on his work. His assignment took him to Sicily, where he met with then-godfather Calogere Vizzini. The purpose of the visit was to establish relationships with Charles Luciano and Godfather Vizzini. There were high-level rumors that the Mafia, infiltrating in America, was now bringing in heroin. When Chinigo questioned Vizzini about his relationship with Luciano, Vizzini said he was familiar with the family name only because they lived in Vizzini's town. But the government knew Luciano and Vizzini were business partners and had previously set up a candy factory in Palermo that exported their product throughout Europe and the United States. Law enforcement thought it was a cover for heroin trafficking. Vizzini stated that he thought the United States "was silly in thinking that the Mafia was a criminal organization." Vizzini said that in every society there is a group of people who solve problems. In America it is the government. In Sicily, problems were solved by "private individuals." Though Vizzini played the role of a common person, it was thought that he was responsible for thirty-nine murders and numerous other criminal acts. Michael's journey was, for the most part, in vain. Don Vizzini refused to make any other comments.[17]

Michael made arrangements to meet with Lucky, who, like Vizzini, would not divulge any knowledge of what Michael was referring to with the word mafia. During the brief meeting between Michael and Luciano, a Hearst photographer did manage to snap a picture of the two, and he put the picture in a report that was published by the Chicago American.[18]

Marajen should have recognized some inconsistencies in Michael's source of income. It was not possible to repair the villa cheaply, especially to Marajen's taste, and a news reporter did not earn what could be called a high-end salary. To keep the villa in condition and maintain the décor Marajen wished to present took lots of money. She furnished many of the rooms with "antiques," accepted as genuine because of Michael's ability to pass off fake antiques as real. Also it's possible that Michael may have dabbled in illegal cigarette and drug trafficking to support Marajen's taste in furnishing. In that era that could easily be done while furniture for Marajen was shipped back and forth from Italy to America. It would be quite easy to plant drugs within the furniture that would not be discovered by customs. Marajen was truly in love with Michael, but she was not educated in fine furnishings. If Michael approved of it, then it was fine with her. Michael had portrayed himself as businessman both in public and to Marajen. Michael would earn the money. The job of looking good or putting on the Ritz was left to Marajen.

Prior to Michael and Marajen's marriage, Helen Stevick had been instrumental in acquiring the first VHF television station in the Champaign area. The newspaper and the attorneys for the paper persuaded the Federal Communications Commission to grant the VHF channel to Champaign in 1952. However, just days earlier, the Lindsey-Schaub newspaper chain out of Decatur, owner of the Urbana Courier newspaper, had also applied. When the problem was discovered, both parties were notified and told that they would have to consolidate their filings, which could mean being stuck in the court system for years before the television channel would be awarded. To avoid this, Decatur-based Illinois Broadcasting Company teamed up with Champaign Midwest Television and its attorney, August Meyer. Mr. Meyer would hold 51 percent, Illinois Broadcasting would hold 20 percent, and the Stevicks and News-Gazette executives would hold the remaining shares. Thus was born WCIA television, the third of five original central Illinois stations. With everyone's approval, Amos and Andy, Captain Kangaroo, The Ed Sullivan Show, and The Honeymooners were now seen in Champaign living rooms. Though the station did well and was flourishing twenty years after its birth, Marajen had to sell the station in 1972 due to a cross-ownership conflict. Marajen sold the station for less than its worth but, again, avoided years of court battles.[19] Had Marajen waited a while, she would have been grandfathered in and not had to sell her shares.

Late in 1954, Marajen was approached by her mother regarding the publisher position at the News-Gazette. Helen was getting older and tired of the day-to-day work the paper demanded. Knowing Marajen's fanciful imagination, Helen was concerned about Marajen being the sole publisher of the News-Gazette. She told Marajen that she wanted Michael to be the primary publisher because of his head for business. Marajen initially threw a seismic tantrum. Once she had cooled down and thought of the advantages, she relinquished her position to become secondary publisher of the newspaper. In that position, she had more time to play and party.

While Michael kept busy at the paper, Marajen made several trips to her villa. On returning from one trip, she told Michael she had received a phone call from Italy stating that they had acquired more property in Italy, but she was not sure of the location. She asked Michael when he had purchased the property and how much he had spent. Michael brushed her off, saying, "It was a gift from a friend or a debt repaid." Marajen never inquired further about the property. Marajen both never put two and two together, or she just didn't care. If some of his dealings were underhanded, she looked away or added the acquisition to her unquenchable thirst for "things."[20]

Most people in Champaign didn't consider Michael the type they figured Marajen would wed. He was short and mousey. He was referred to by many as a con artist. He couldn't carry on a conversation on the level she did and would drift away at parties. He didn't have a driver's license and was notorious for walking wherever he had to go in town.

Other people found Michael charming. The newspaper staff respected him. He never failed to speak to them in the morning, and he actually held the paper together during the rough years. Michael was always very well-dressed, including Italian shoes and monogrammed shirts and expensive ties. He spent long hours writing the editorials and straightening out problems. He assisted Helen Stevick in designing the new building addition, which included a new pressroom and warehouse. What impressed the staff was that Michael even helped to set up the new three-story high press that was purchased in Chicago and brought to Champaign.

But to the News-Gazette administration, he didn't fit in well in Champaign. When he and Marajen were at the Stevick home on Prospect Avenue, he would walk to Charles Wesley's home on Springfield and play gin the better part of the day. The administration felt Michael didn't spend enough time at the paper. He might spend hours in his office, but no one knew exactly what he was doing. His door was usually closed. With little notice he would tell Marajen to take control of the routine paper business for weeks on end while he went to Italy to tend to business there. It is believed that Michael had a deeper involvement with the Mafia than Marajen would admit to. It was suspected that his frequent trips to Italy were on Mafia business, under the guise of reporting. When Michael did return he always had large amounts of money on him. Some thought he was laundering Mafia money through the News-Gazette and neither Marajen nor Helen were aware of it.

Both the Chinigo's wished for warmer climates to vacation in when time didn't accommodate trips to Italy. On a visit to California, they found a house outside of Los Angeles that Michael thought would be perfect for them. Michael purchased the ranch, intending to surprise Marajen with it. Michael may have thought it a perfect getaway, but Marajen was furious. She called it a rundown shack and said she wouldn't be caught dead in it. Thinking Marajen would eventually grow to like it, he maintained it for several months. Marajen never stepped foot in it, and Michael sold it months later.

Even with his close involvement with the News-Gazette, Michael kept his retainer with Hearst Publishers in California.

While working on reporting assignments in California for Hearst, Michael met Doris Duke. An heiress to a tobacco and electric energy fortune, Duke took a job as a writer for Hearst under the supervision of Michael Chinigo. After Duke was introduced to Marajen, the two women found they had much in common. Both women commanded power and often formed social relationships with powerful people. Both were possessive and often openly jealous of someone who was or was perceived to be a threat to a relationship. The two women often found humor in rebelling against rules, and neither liked to give in to outside authority. Marajen thought being seen with Doris Duke would only enhance the stellar image she had of herself.

But Michael had the personality Doris felt most comfortable with, and the two of them became lasting friends. Both could be found in clubs and restaurants together and at lunches and dinners without Marajen. Of course Doris's notoriety also brought out the paparazzi, and soon the gossip trail began. The tabloids hinted that Doris was having an intimate relationship with Michael. Though Doris never admitted to this, Marajen dropped her as a friend and refused to have the name Doris Duke mentioned around her. Years later Duke started the Doris Duke American Indian Oral History Program, which was initiated in several state universities. The University of Illinois in Champaign was one school that participated in the program. Duke's goal in the project was to collect first-hand testimony from Native Americans on Indian issues. In spite of Marajen's feelings, Michael stayed close friends with Doris and was the executor of her will.

# The Bay of Pigs

In the 1950s, Havana, Cuba, was fast becoming the Monte Carlo of the Caribbean, but trouble was brewing in this lascivious, corrupt country. Johnny Rosselli had been making trips to Cuba for the purpose of checking on the high-rise casinos and brothels that had been started and financed by the Mob. Johnny would also check the accountant's books to verify what profits were coming out of the casinos to be sent to Chicago and Vegas. On one trip, Johnny took Bill and Judy Campbell. Bill Campbell was under contract with Warner Brothers film studio and knew Johnny well through the motion picture industry. Johnny, forever the playboy, found Judy to be quite beautiful and enjoyed being seen in her company, even if her husband had to come along. Her marriage to Bill was coming apart, and Johnny's flirting with her on this trip offered nothing to mend the marriage. Judy Campbell, of course, is remembered as a mistress of John Kennedy, but she was a childhood friend of Rosselli's, and the friendship lasted for decades.

Casino Nacional, started by Meyer Lansky, was a beautifully built complex with bars, gaming rooms, and restaurants. Cuban casinos brought in Hollywood stars for top billing. At the Nacional, Eartha Kitt was the star of the floor show. Top show stars enticed groves of international tourists, ready to spend their money, to the hotels, beaches, and nightclubs.

Cuban dictator Fulgencio Batista y Zaldivar had a close friendship with Lansky and approved of the casinos, which both brought income into the country and forged a powerful hold for the Mafia. Batista was looking only to secure his role as dictator, but the Mob had set their sights on sharing the power in equal portions. In other words, Batista would own the country of Cuba, but it would be under Mob rule. Because of the constant flow of money, it wasn't long before other casinos were up and running. First the Capri, then the Havana Hilton, which was run by Cliff Jones, former lieutenant governor of Nevada, were erected. The famous Cuban Riviera was managed by Rosselli's friend Charlie Baron. At the Riviera, Ginger Rogers headlined with comedians Abbot and Costello.

Though Johnny was on business in Cuba, he behaved like a relaxed vacationer. The FBI wasn't making a nuisance of themselves by tailing him. Because Johnny brought high rollers to Havana, he became a friend of Batista.

The cunning Rosselli was making a reliable name for himself with the upper levels of the Mafia. He had already earned the respect and favors of Santo Trafficante Jr., the Florida godfather who had a huge financial investment in Cuba.

The Florida Don's father, Santo Sr., had been the figurehead in establishing the casinos in Cuba. He had negotiated with Meyer Lansky and other Mafia heads in choosing Havana for the casino enterprise. In the mid 1940s both Trafficantes were added to the FBI narcotics division wanted list, when it was proved that both had financed heroin shipments from Cuba to New York City. When Santo Trafficate Sr. died in August 1954, Santo Jr. was given the title of Mafia head in both Florida and in Cuba. This firmly established Rosselli's position in Cuba.

Rosselli's cozy relationship with the Florida Mafia head was fine for his Mafia resume, but it also opened doors for unwanted attention. Once again the United States government, particularly the CIA, focused their interest on Rosselli. But keeping up with Rosselli was not a piece of cake. Johnny, not new to the spy world, was a very secretive person in accordance with his training in his chosen profession. If the CIA wanted solid information as to what Rosselli was up to, it would take lots of work and a diligent agent to get it. Johnny rarely made phone calls for business deals or contacts. He spoke in person and knew when to keep his mouth shut. He also had a keen nose; he knew when he was being followed and had a knack for loosing a tail.

The small island of Cuba was experiencing governmental problems. The current ruler, Fulgencio Batista, had become unpopular with the inhabitants due to rampant corruption. A lawyer and military person, Fidel Castro and his military forces had for years planned an overthrow of Bastista's dictatorship. The U.S. government, aware of Castro's intentions, sided, to a degree, with Castro. His plan was to run the country under a socialist form of government. The United States withheld total support, knowing full well that Castro had aligned himself with the USSR. Communism was spreading and now reached the tiny island of Cuba. Castro's plan of implementing new social and economic programs did not convince the United States. They smelled Communism in disguise. By the mid 1950s President Eisenhower had severed ties with Batista. The Cuban Revolution erupted in 1953, and Fidel Castro was in power.

Emissaries from the Mob met with the new ruler, who attempted to assure them that on the business level, nothing would change except that the monetary cut from the casinos would now be 60-40 in Cuba's favor, no longer 50-50 as under Batista. Communism was spreading and now touching the tiny island of Cuba. Castro's plan of implementing new social and economic programs did not convince the United States. They smelled Communism in disguise.

The United States government wasn't happy with the

new Cuban ruler. There was already talk among government officials that Castro needed to be eliminated from power. The U.S. government knew who was funding the entertainment in Cuba and who was profiting from it. The situation had to stop for financial reasons and Castro, being a communist, had to go for political reasons.

In October 1960, the Gaceta Official de la Republic de Cuba confiscated the Havana Rivera Hotel and Casino and ran the owners out of the country. Seeing an extremely lucrative business gone, Rosselli and other Mafia members became receptive to the overthrow of Castro and surreptitiously offered their services in surreptitiously to the CIA. Interested parties made numerous assassination attempts, including using a pesticide such as thallium salts, subjecting Castro's cigars to biological substances, and lacing a diver's suit with a deadly bacteria and then presenting the suit to Castro as a gift. These plans either didn't work or were snuffed before implementation. There were also rumors that the CIA approached Trafficante to take Castro out, and Trafficante gave every indication that he already had a team in position to do this, when in reality he would do no such thing for financial reasons.

Early in the Kennedy administration, the CIA suggested that the president meet with a particular CIA agent who had a golden record with several security-sensitive cases: William Harvey. Bill Harvey had begun to formulate a way to rid Cuba of Castro during the later years of the Eisenhower administration.

The idea of using a member or members of the Mafia in an assassination plot against Castro developed in early 1960. It is thought that Harvey was instructed by President John Kennedy to get rid of Castro, plain and simple. But at no time did Kennedy ever concede his knowledge of a plot. Kennedy knew full well about a mission to overthrow Castro's government. Since Bill Harvey was put in charge of the mission, Kennedy had to have understood the ultimate goal, because Harvey's reputation was that of a top spy who plotted the assassination of foreign leaders.

Early in 1960 Bill Harvey flew from Washington, D.C., to Miami in order to be introduced to Johnny Rosselli, who would plan and assist in removing Fidel Castro from power. The two men hit it off immediately. Both were strongly anti-communist, and for whatever reason, their personalities blended. Harvey named the newest plot against Castro Phase II. When Harvey disclosed to Rosselli what was needed, Rosselli seemed shocked that the CIA would consider him to take care of the problem. The feds were, once again, stalking him, and now they wanted him to help them. With a few moments to think about the job, Rosselli recognized a personal benefit in it. If he assisted the government in eliminating the Communist leader, he would then have leverage if the government attempted to prosecute him over gambling. The CIA offered Rosselli payment for the job, but Rosselli refused, requesting only that his expenses be paid.

A few weeks later Rosselli put Harvey and one of Harvey's close associates in contact with Sam Giancana from Chicago. He and two other mobsters decided that pills would be placed in Castro's tea by an unnamed woman who was close to Castro. Of course when the Oval Office got wind of the plot that involved mobsters, it was shut down and the pills were returned to Giancana. For one reason or another, the mission of eliminating Castro was not being accomplished, and Harvey began to lose favor with his superiors.

Robert Kennedy, who had already had a run-in with Harvey, found out that Harvey was behind the pill plot, and he contacted the head of the CIA, demanding that Bill Harvey be pulled out of the field and shoved behind a desk somewhere. Indeed Bill Harvey was shut down in the United States and sent to Rome. The CIA made it clear that Harvey's contacts with Rosselli were to be for the sake of homeland security only.

The threat was clear enough to chill public contact between Rosselli and Harvey, but the two stayed friends.

While Bill Harvey worked on small jobs for the CIA in Rome, Johnny trotted back to Vegas and met up with Jeanne Carman, another Hollywood sexpot, who had divorced her husband in 1958. Johnny escorted Jeanne to a party at the Sands hosted by Frank Sinatra. Also in attendance were Elvis, Dean Martin, Jerry Lewis, Marilyn Monroe, Joan Crawford, and Marajen Chinigo. Marajen was unaware that Johnny would be at the party. Joan Crawford had invited Marajen and insisted that she attend. Jeanne, still trying to make it big in the movies, clung to Rosselli when Johnny approached Marajen. For once Marajen acted like a lady. She spoke with Johnny and Jeanne, keeping the topics social. Lurking in the shadows at a distance table were singer Phyllis McGuire and Johnny's old friend Sam Giancana, Chicago's underworld boss. By now Johnny felt he had the best of both worlds. He was a wealthy Mob boss in Vegas and, to a degree, in Cuba. Just a few weeks earlier he had been handed a contract by the U.S. government to eliminate Fidel Castro. Everybody loved Johnny.[21]

By his third wedding anniversary, Michael Chinigo was putting the finishing touches on his book; The Teachings of Pope Pius XII (Methuen, London, 1958). The book pertained to the political slant during the reign of Pius XII. In the book, Chinigo projects, strongly, the Vatican's power on world events, as well as the domestic duties of husbands and wives. Marajen enjoyed her time in Rome while Michael wrote. She even escaped to meet with friends in California and, on one occasion, Cuba. During the approximately four-week vacation, Marajen toured Columbia, South America, and finally met up with Rosselli in Cuba for the last few days. How she connected with Rosselli is unclear. Some sources said he contacted her, and others said she wired friends in California who then contacted him.

A former dignitary from Germany stated that he remembered Marajen and Johnny entering a casino in Cuba during that vacation and the stir the jeweled gown Marajen wore caused. "An elegant, absolutely lovely lady she was! Mr. Rosselli was equally dashing in his silk suit. They looked like storybook characters from fantasy land. They walked up to a roulette table, and she played $100 dollars on a number. She lost and they walked away." The dignitary noticed how captivating Marajen was. Waiters would circle Marajen and Johnny as if they were royalty. They dined and danced for hours, and in the early morning light retired to a hotel.

While browsing the Spanish antique shops in Cuba, Marajen met up with America's sweetheart, Joan Crawford. Joan was in Cuba with an unknown male companion, and Marajen invited her to a late lunch at her hotel. The two ladies spent the rest of the day together, touring the city of Havana. Later that evening both ladies attended a dinner party that included one of Castro's mistresses. The mistress had a sinewy teenage son, with whom Marajen, using her sexual prowess, managed to have a one night stand before she left the tiny country.[22]

Her vacation over, Marajen returned to her villa in Italy. She was in a party mood to celebrate Michael's book publication. Parties were Marajen's forte, and her reputation for lavish parties was already well-known throughout Italy. Those attending were mostly from Italy and Greece. They were greeted poolside by numerous naked young maidens and effeminate young males. Names on her guest list were often not well-known to Marajen, so she would memorize their names, positions, and biographies. The guests that she could not house at the villa were housed in rooms she rented for them at the San Pietro Hotel in Salerno, Italy. A few of the guests were friends of Michael's, but the majorities were power hitters from Naples, Salerno, and Rome. When Marajen spoke to her guests about her lengthy vacation, Cuba was not mentioned, nor was the fact that she had spent time with Johnny Rosselli. She only talked of the countryside, business-related subjects, and the movie stars she had met.

Michael was seen at the party but drifted away after initial pleasantries.

The Chinigo's eventually settled into married life. A vineyard was started on acreage on their villa above the Gulf of Salerno. Gardens and reflecting pools were designed and landscaped by both of them. Fig, olive, and cypress trees were planted in groomed beds of fertile soil. By all outward appearance they seemed a normal married couple. Shopping in Salerno and surrounding cities brought more antiques and artifacts into the home. Marajen spent spare time painting landscapes and the town of Ravello that rested below their villa.

While Marajem was living high with her parties, Johnny Rosselli was lying low and avoiding the CIA and FBI. He just did what he had to do with the Vegas casinos and off-and-on meetings in Florida with Trafficante. The word among the crime families of Sam Giancana, Santo Trafficante, Meyer Lansky, and Carlos Marcello was that a Democrat was causing a stir in the country that might not be good for their business. Johnny Rosselli was ordered to gather the available information and take it to the godfathers who had the most to lose if the rumors were true.

*Marajen Stevick in her 20's*

*Marajen Stevick with her father in the late 1020s*

*"I grew up sharing his desk and he yearned to teach me all he had learned." Marajen Stevick Chinigo telling about her father, David Stevick, who created The News-Gazette newspaper in Champaign, Illinois*

*Marajen Stevick Chinigo with her mother Helen,*
*on vacation in Venice, 1955.*

*Mrs. Marajen Stevick Dyess plays cards with her third husband, Edwin*
*Dysee on the train from W. Virginia to Chicago, Illinois. A lieutenant*
*colonel in the U.S. Army Air Force he escaped from a Japanese POW camp*
*after surviving the Bataan Death March. He died while test piloting a*
*plane on December 22,1943. Mrs. Chinigo died 59 years later to the day.*

*Marajen Stevick interviews U.S. Representative D.C. Dobbins, a*
*Champaign Democrat, in the newly opened WDWS studio in 1937. The*
*station was located on the second floor of the News-Gazette building in*
*downtown Champaign*

*Mrs. Marajen Chinigo with late husband, Michael Chinigo at a social function. Mr.Chinigo was a war correspondent and director of the International News Services in Italy. In 1954 he became associate publisher of The News-Gazette, a position he held for many years. According to Rome police he died of a self-inflicted gunshot wound.*

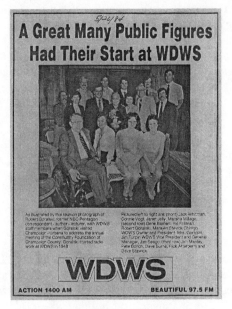

*WDWS staff photo taken in 1984*

*Mrs. Marajen Chinigo at home in Champaign, IL
with her beloved poodles.*

*Marajen Chinigo painted at her villa in Italy.*

*Dining room at Marajen Chinigo's home in Champaign, Il.*

*Marajen Chinigo in her own personal 'car.'*

*Sam Giancano was supposed to have testified about the plot against Castro, but was assassinated by 6 .22-caliber bullets in June, 1975. The murder was never solved.*

*Johnny Rosselli after testifying in 1975. He was to testify again but his cut up body was found floating in an oil can off the coast of Florida. His murder was never solved.*

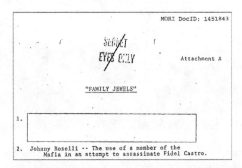

*CIA sheet on Johnny Rosselli. Note the various spellings he went under.*

May the light of      E.SPecially Yours      (309) 244-8515
love surround you      *Greta Alexander*      P.O. Box 664
                       Parapsychologist      Delavan, IL 61734

*Greta Alexander. Marajen Chinigo was just one of Greta Alexander's famous clients. Marajen insisted on a reading the day her husband, Michael, was shot.*

*Mrs. Marajen Chinigo at a company Christmas party December 13, 2002. Mrs.Chinigo regarded her employees as her family.*

# The Kennedy Connection

The new man in the publicity arena in the United States was a senior senator from Massachusetts by the name of John Kennedy, a vibrant, handsome man whose voice was being heard across the country. John Kennedy was a man of prestige, wealth, and appealing ideals that hit the voting populace by storm. But the Kennedy name wasn't new to the Mafia. His father, Joseph Kennedy, had been in bed with the Mafia during the stock market crash. The New York Mob made sure Kennedy's investments were secure, enriching the Kennedy fortune.

Before that Joe Kennedy was heavily involved in illegal booze. He considered his illegal risks as important as his legal businesses. He didn't take risks without giving serious thought to each one of them. He was one of the liquor haulers who brought illegal whiskey from Canada to Lake Erie to be distributed in Chicago and down-state Illinois. He sought out the Mafia's help, specifically Al Capone, for this early deal. What Capone hadn't realized was Kennedy was making a deal to sell his whiskey.

Joe Kennedy had played golf with Rosselli and dined with members of the Chicago outfit at the Cal-Nev Lodge in Lake Tahoe. The purpose of the dinner was a thank you from Dean Martin, Peter Lawford, and Frank Sinatra. They now had a lucrative gambling business thanks to the Nevada Mafia. When approached by attorneys for the East Coast family, Joe Kennedy offered financial support for the Hotel Nacional in Havana and was a hidden partner in the ownership of the Desert Inn in Vegas. Joe didn't miss a beat when it came to finding ways to make money. The problem was, it didn't matter if it was legal or not. For Joe Kennedy the majority of the business deals were not.

When son John was running a close second to Richard Nixon in the pre-election months, patriarch Joe Kennedy met with Giancana in a Chicago hotel. Joe needed the Mob's help to swing West Virginia to the Kennedy ticket. In exchange, Joe Kennedy promised that if Jack were elected president, he and his brother Bobby would go easy on the Mob. It was a hush-hush deal; Joe Kennedy couldn't afford rumors to leak about that agreement or any of the other Mob-connected deals he had been apart of. In essence, it was "scratch my back, and I'll scratch yours," but in truth Joe Kennedy sold his son to the Mob.

Cuba was still a hotbed after John Kennedy was elected to the White House. Plots and plans to oust Fidel Castro continued. Each time Kennedy rejected them. Each time the plans were shelved. It was finally decided, after months of planning, to go into Cuba militarily. It was felt that the aggressive guerrilla force, numbering over 1,500, gathered at the Bay of Pigs on the south coast of Cuba could overthrow the Communist dictator with United States' military support. The United States was supposed to offer both land and sea support. The goal was to rid Cuba of Castro, his brother Raul, and their regime. This was intended as a surprise, but the Cuban government had been warned ahead of the invasion by the KGB and instead of a victory for the United Sates and the Cubans, it became known as the botched paramilitary invasion of Cuba. Thousands of Cuban revolutionaries were killed or imprisoned. The CIA was prepared to accept its role in the blundered invasion. It even wiped the egg off its face to maintain the secret that the Mafia was partners with the CIA in the plot. It is believed that Kennedy knew of the Mafia's involvement but never, in plain language, conceded that knowledge.

Through 1961, Rosselli spent most of his time outside of the United States. Late in September 1962, Rosselli returned to Vegas and dined with friends at the Star Dust. Johnny was causally asked where he had been for so long. Johnny responded, "Miami on business."

Someone else added, "Probably chasing skirts and running from husbands!" Everyone laughed but Johnny. He turned to the man and very coldly replied, "I said business." He then stood, threw some money on the table, and left.[23] Johnny's dimmed mood was largely due to his frustration over the failed attempts on Castro's life. That certainly was reason enough, but there was another reason Johnny's mood had changed.

Even after the Bay of Pigs, plans to overthrow Castro continued. At some undisclosed place in Miami in the fall of 1962, Bill Harvey met with Rosselli. At this meeting Harvey learned that the deadly pills were still in Cuba, safely hidden. At that time Rosselli was unaware that a new crisis was beginning, involving Russia and Cuba. It would soon be picked up by the news media and labeled the Cuban Missile Crisis.

October 15, 1962, after the Bay of Pigs, Robert Kennedy had been told by CIA operatives still stationed in Cuba, that weapons were being moved into Cuba by the KGB. He had been assured by the Russians that the weapons were for defense only. To confirm this, the president sent the United States' newest spy plane, the U-2, to retrieve information on the situation. It took the pilot only six minutes to take 928 photos that proved medium-range missiles and eight missile transporters were en route to Cuba, capable of reaching various points in the United States. President Kennedy was now faced with two problems: making the untrained eye of the American people believe what the photos showed, and the possible military action that might be required. The failed Bay of Pigs incident still lingered in peoples' memories, and the president was still experiencing the embarrassment. Convincing the American people of a potential crisis was not going to be easy.

Realizing the eminent danger to his country, as well as other countries in the free world, Kennedy chose to impose a navel blockade against the Soviet ships carrying missile-building equipment and missiles to Cuba. President Kennedy also informed Russia that under no circumstances would the United States sit back and let this continue. The Soviet ships, seeing what they were up against, requested immediate orders from the Soviet Union on what to do. Khrushchev ordered the Soviet ships to turn around and return home. This ended the crisis and averted a nuclear war.

With world events thus tempered, the Kennedy administration once again focused on national issues. Attorney General Robert Kennedy was telling of his war on organized crime. The Mafia was upset with what they heard. They had offered their services more than once with the Cuban situation and the Kennedy administration let it be known they wanted nothing to do with a Mafia-orchestrated assassination.

Now Robert Kennedy spoke openly against them. He had several high-level Mafia figureheads under constant watch by his men. He was trying to prosecute Santo Trafficante and Carlos Marcello, as neither were United States citizens. If Kennedy could get a conviction on both of them, even minor ones, both would be deported. Trafficante went ballistic and wanted to know why Joe Kennedy had not kept his word once the Mafia made sure John was in the oval office. Joe earnestly tried to convince Bobby and Jack to go easy on organized crime, but both sons refused. Sam Giancana was incensed over the deteriorating relationship between the Kennedys and some of the well-known movie stars.

Sammy Davis Jr. had been asked to postpone his wedding to actress Mai Britt until after the election. He did so out of respect for his friends Jack and Jackie. When invitations went out for the inaugural ball, Sammy wasn't invited. While in California on government business Jack had agreed to stay at Frank Sinatra's home in Palm Springs. Sinatra made lavish renovations to his home and borrowed some of Marajen Chinigo's antiques for one occasion. Marajen also made suggestions on menu ideas for the Kennedys. When the time came for Jack and Jackie to arrive, Jack made a change and stayed at Bing Crosby's home. These stars were the same people who donated their time and money to campaign for John Kennedy; this snubbing by the Kennedys seemed arrogant. To ice the cake of Kennedy dissatisfaction, it was learned that Sam Giancana and John Kennedy were sharing the same girl friend, Judith Campbell. Judith was already friends with the famous Rat Pack thanks to Frank Sinatra. Maintaining the brotherhood, Sinatra passed her on to Sam Giancana. To stay in good with the high-ranking political figures, Sinatra introduced her to John Kennedy in early 1960. Because of her connection with the underworld Kennedy used her to win votes from people with Mafia influence in the presidential pre-election days.

But it was Bobby Kennedy's seething hatred and vowed promise to rid the nation of organized crime that put Santo Trafficante over the edge. He let it be known that John Kennedy was done and went so far as to say there would be a hit.[24]

In the early spring of 1963, Johnny Rosselli made an unexpected stop in Champaign. Marajen, aware that he was coming, had released most of her staff that evening and answered the door herself. Johnny spoke with Marajen in soft tones as they sipped drinks. Johnny's friend, Frank Sinatra, had recently sponsored him for a membership in the upscale Los Angeles Friar's Club, and Johnny eagerly passed the news on to Marajen. Later, Johnny told Marajen he had concocted a card-game operation at the club. He was scooping in thousands of dollars from well-known members. The name dropping pleased Marajen, and she recounted specific times she had had with each of them. This new card game later proved to be a scam, but Marajen couldn't see the illegal side of it. Marajen expressed her happiness with the Friar's Club's acceptance. She spent the rest of their time talking of her travels and plans for another trip to California in the near future. Learning this, Johnny suggested she stay in Champaign for a few more weeks. He would not be able to be with her socially in California because he "would be gone for some time on important business and she shouldn't be around." Marajen, knowing Johnny intimately, felt comfortable asking Johnny what the business was and if it had to do with the Friar's Club. Rosselli shook his head and said it was better that she didn't know should she be questioned afterwards. Before Marajen could say more, Johnny took her hands in his, kissed her on the cheek, wished her well, and left.[25]

# A Shock Wave
# Shakes the World

Neither the Bay of Pigs nor the Cuban Missile Crisis stopped the Mafia from plotting to eliminate Castro. Selected organized crime figures began supplying Cuban exiles with arms and ammunition to dethrone the leader. President Kennedy denounced these plans, saying that sabotage plans against Castro had totally ceased. Kennedy did assign more navy planes and customs boats to patrol the Straits of Florida. Behind the scenes, the Kennedy administration was secretly planning a coup in Cuba. A possible military action against Cuba to end the Castro regime was to be headed by Robert Kennedy and carried out by the Defense Department-a possible military action against Cuba to end the Castro regime of the country. Only a few government agencies understood the particulars of the plans. John and Robert Kennedy's goal was not so much an assassination plot but a thoroughly thought-out plan for the Cuban people to overthrow the dictator. The Kennedys knew this had to be done right, or it could trigger another faceoff with Russia.

In spite of the ill-fated military action, the shadows of the Camelot mystique remained with the American people.

The romance, the chivalry, and the pomp and ceremony still cast a spell three years after the inaugural ball. But once again an underground group of people were not looking at things through the same rose-colored glasses as most of the American people.

During the summer of 1963, Rosselli had dinner with Bill Harvey on the East Coast. The FBI, maintaining an antenna on Rosselli, knew of the meeting. Harvey was on his way to Rome with the blessings of Robert Kennedy and others. He had been instructed to disassociate himself from Rosselli. It is believed by sources that at this final meeting Rosselli hinted to Harvey that something big was going down soon, because Santo Trafficante and Carlos Marcello were mad as hell with Bobby Kennedy.[26]

By whatever means, the underworld got wind of the plan. The Mafia was still fuming over the loss of income from the Cuban casinos and the Kennedy administration's focus on the war to end organized crime. They had been badly burnt on both counts. Trafficante, Marcello, and Rosselli considered what Robert Kennedy's unrelenting persecution of them an act of vengeance. The Justice Department had not relented in looking for ways to deport Carlos Marcello, godfather of New Orleans. In fact they did manage to have him deported for a brief time. Trafficante could not let go of the fact that he and Sam Giancana put Jack Kennedy in the White House, with the understanding that the government would lighten up on them and a few others. Santo Trafficante spoke with Carlos Marcello and Johnny Rosselli in late summer of 1963 in Miami. Santo had an agenda of his own that could be covered up by the new Cuban coup plans. Trafficante wanted Jack killed. Marcello couldn't agree more, for much the same reasons, and Rosselli wanted to move up in rank. Jack Kennedy was going to be in Dallas in November. Someone else would be too.

Carlos Marcello knew of a man who, for the most part, was disillusioned with the American system of government, particularly the Justice and Defense Departments. A marksman out to make a name for himself, he had flirted with Communism and dabbled with low-level crime figures. That man was Lee Harvey Oswald. When Oswald was approached by a caller sent by Marcello to do Marcello a favor, Oswald jumped at the chance. He knew the perfect spot in Dallas: the School Book Depository building that overlooked Dealey Plaza. Marcello's people agreed. But Oswald wasn't the only one requested to be of service to the Mafia in this operation. Oswald was only to serve as another layer of protection or cover for the one who would actually carry out the order. Giancana had Jack Ruby of Chicago, another wannabe big shot, prepped for a job. Giancana's people told Ruby a lunatic would be blamed for the crime, but Ruby had to get to Oswald before he revealed his real position in the plan. Ruby, agreeing to carry this out, received a large monetary payment in advance.

The heavy hitter of concern here is Johnny Rosselli. After a series of meetings that spanned the continent, to throw off the CIA and the FBI, the planners put their players in position. Rosselli, who liked President Kennedy, was uncomfortable with his role in the plan but didn't have a choice. The plan was in place. All that was left was the action.

An unidentified woman drove Rosselli from Miami to Dallas. Early on the morning of November 22, Rosselli casually walked through a large drain culvert that wound its way under Dealey Plaza in Dallas, Texas. A gun had already been placed there for him. He positioned himself in such a way that he could see the presidential motorcade from the street drain that went out onto the Plaza. No one would see him, as they would be looking toward the black, open limousine carrying the president and his wife, Jackie. He would see them from the front. He had one chance and one shot.[27]

After the event that shocked the world on November 22, 1963, Johnny remained out of circulation for several weeks. He didn't want the CIA or the FBI to even dream that he had been in Dallas. Johnny purposely stayed away from the public eye. But while he was getting a grip on his own life, he found some comfort in the fact that because Jack Kennedy was out of the picture, Robert Kennedy's personal war with the Mafia was dead! Until the dust settled, he spent long hours at the Friar's Club dining with friends like George Burns and Milton Berle. After a few weeks, Rosselli was noticed at his usual haunts, always with a girl on his arm …if not two. He seemed very carefree, not looking over his shoulder. He made sure he was seen by people who knew him well.

During this time he enjoyed an evening with Marajen, who was visiting friends from San Francisco. Leaving Milton Berle's table, Johnny went over to Marajen and her friends. Johnny whispered in her ear, and Marajen immediately stood up and excused herself, and the pair left the dinning area. Under the cover of trees Johnny placed both hands on Marajen's arms. Though the conversation could not be heard, Johnny seemed to be telling Marajen something very important. Marajen was observed putting a hand to her mouth; seconds later she left Johnny in a rush. At that point Marajen returned to a table that included couples she knew, but she remained silent. She did not see Johnny anymore that evening. A few weeks later Johnny seemed to have changed his attitude about things. Something was bothering him. He was distant and quiet. It is believed that he placed a few calls to Marajen via pay phones, but no conversations resulted from these calls. Whether Marajen refused to talk to him or she wasn't available is not known. He even visited a priest for confessions a few times. After the Kennedy assassination, Johnny made one trip to Chicago late in 1963 to meet with Sam Giancana, who was being visited by Judy Campbell.[28] It is unclear what the purpose of the meeting was.

Marajen was home in Champaign working at the News-Gazette. Rosselli called her from Chicago. Only Marajen's side was heard and that was said in a whispered voice. Johnny was in trouble and needed someone to talk to. He called Marajen off and on at her home in Champaign in the early spring of 1964, and they lunched a couple of times between 1964 and 1966, when Marajen could get away and fly to California. Though it looked like Johnny was staying out of trouble, he wasn't. The rigged card game Dapper Johnny had put together a few years earlier was seeing a lot of action in the back rooms of the Friar's Club. Johnny's role was to bring in high rollers, who included Debbie Reynolds' husband, Harry Karl, Phil Silvers, and Zeppo Marx. Eventually members from the Detroit and St. Louis crime families showed up. Rosselli rarely played, but he made it clear he was to get his cut first. Before the scam was uncovered, Harry Karl had lost everything, and Marx didn't fair much better. A short time later the Feds caught on. On December 2, 1968, Johnny was indicted, convicted, and fined $55,000 for his role in the card game scam. It is estimated that Rosselli's cut was around $400,000.00. In addition to this conviction, he also served six months on earlier immigration charges. Life was getting harder for Johnny. The Feds were onto his scams. The one person in his life he truly loved and trusted, his beloved mother, had just died. Rosselli, devastated with the news was released from prison long enough to attend his mother's funeral on the East Coast. When Robert Kennedy was assassinated on the West Coast Rosselli found the tragedy a call for celebration. After his mother's funeral, Johnny served part of his prison term in a Northwest prison, but due to his health he finished his sentence in a Santa Barbara, California, prison.

With Rosselli imprisoned, Marajen renewed her friendship with Joan Crawford. To satisfy her whim for doing things off the cuff, Marajen booked a jet for a shopping trip in New York. The two women took a break from shopping to attend Andrew Crispo's art gallery opening on East 57th Street and Madison. How they happened to know Crispo is not clear or who made the arrangements for them to be included on the guest list at the opening is not clear.

Marajen had dabbled in the bohemian lifestyle, maybe to escape her own, and enjoyed the freedom from inhibitions of the scantily dressed and scandalously well-built gay artists at the opening. The promising artist was first to break open the counterculture lifestyle of some artists by discreetly maintaining a normal store front for his gallery but holding wild sadomasochistic sex and drug parties on the inside. Neighbors had complained to the police with their suspicions of what was happening, but Crispo's payoffs to police and government officials allowed the activities to continue. Neither Marajen nor Joan participated in the activities but enjoyed their positions as voyeurs. Marajen especially enjoyed Joan's shock at the counterculture. They were introduced to Crispo when one of his friends recognized Joan. The two women shared drinks and conversation late into the night with Crispo and three of his closest friends. This was followed by another day of shopping before the ladies returned to Illinois. Marajen chose not to reveal their adventure to anyone in Champaign.

Few businesses accepted openly gay people during the '60s. In Greenwich Village in New York, the Stonewall Inn, which was mafia-owned, was the hot spot for gay and lesbian patrons. Andrew Crispo and many others like him wanted society to accept their lifestyle. But society wasn't ready for the lifestyle to be public. Police that hadn't been paid off would wait outside for patrons to exit the Stonewall Inn and beat unsuspecting gay men. Most of them never reported the beatings and those that did never had their cases come to trial. Crispo was later charged with the brutal death of Eigil Vesti, a Norwegian fashion student.

Paroled in 1973, Johnny Rosselli immediately moved to southern Florida to be with family, which included his sister with whom he was very close. Late in 1973, when Johnny once again had a grip on his life, he went to visit Bill Harvey in

Indianapolis, Indiana. Bill had retired from the CIA and the FBI and was trying hard to just be a husband and father. His retirement wasn't something he wanted, but he left the agency with the blessings of his superiors. On the side, Bill dabbled in some attorney work for a few clients. Johnny needed a favor and, looking to Bill for assistance, had his sister contact Bill. He wanted to see an old girlfriend of his in Champaign. Bill agreed to chauffeur him there.

As the perfect hostess, Marajen, expecting Johnny, greeted both Bill and Johnny with open arms. It is believed that Bill and Marajen had met at least twice previously at her villa in the early 1970s. The visits appeared to be of a non-business nature. Rosselli had, no doubt, told Harvey about Marajen, and when Harvey was assigned to the Rome office, he probably went to see her at her villa. After refreshments, the purpose of the journey was approached. Johnny needed money. He knew law enforcement agencies were still hounding him. During his time in prison, new faces were added to the agency's rolls, and Johnny believed these new faces were following him. His income from his rackets was being held by Giancana and two other Mafioso. He couldn't yet get to the funds discreetly. He requested a loan from Marajen of $50,000, which would do until things could get back to normal. Marajen and Johnny talked of the purpose for the money while Bill Harvey sat in another room. Marajen didn't seem concerned about the amount or the reason Johnny needed it. The request was granted, and Marajen provided cash. Though not a financial wizard, Marajen knew cash didn't leave a paper trail. And Johnny couldn't cash a check anywhere. When the business of the meeting was over, Bill Harvey asked Marajen how Michael was. He and Michael knew each other through Rome contacts. Rosselli did not inquire as to Michael's well-being. Once the deal was secured, Johnny and Bill left Champaign.

A few months later Michael and Marajen returned to Italy to consult with an architect and master tradesmen about renovating another area of the villa. They also purchased a new car in Ravello. Driving home from Ravello, an accident occurred which cost a small child its life. Marajen, not being an Italian citizen, would probably been sentenced to prison if convicted of manslaughter. To prevent arrest, Marajen talked a male friend in the vehicle into admitting that he was driving when the accident happened. It was rumored that Marajen paid the man $10,000 to cover for her.[29] Shortly after the accident, Marajen received word from Champaign that Helen had taken a bad fall, breaking her hip. Michael went back to Champaign immediately and took charge of the News-Gazette and Helen's personal responsibilities. The recovery took longer than the doctors thought it should, and they recommended Helen be admitted to a local nursing home to finish her convalescence. Marajen, far too busy at her villa and not wanting to come home, stayed in Italy, and Michael signed the papers to have Helen admitted.

In Marajen's absence at the News-Gazette, Michael had authority to make important decisions. Such authority included overseeing the Rantoul Press newspaper, which was a subsidiary of the News-Gazette.

The Rantoul Press carried local news and some national news concerning Chanute Air Force base. When a new printing press was needed, a well respected employee of the News-Gazette, Steve Farruggia, went to Chicago with Michael and other administrators of the paper for the purchase. Steve and others installed the new press, and the Rantoul Press was back in business. All went well until the FBI, tipped off by an anonymous person, walked in and asked to see the general manager. With a search warrant in hand they began to search the equipment, including the new press. Apparently the manager felt that, when not printing newspapers in Rantoul, he could use the equipment to print money.[30]

# The Paper Business in 1970

In the early 1970s the News-Gazette headlines included topics that had plagued people for years. Racism was still a key topic with corporate businesses and various neighborhoods in large cities. Even after the Civil Rights Act was instituted, the aftermath of the riots left a heavy cloud in some areas of the nation.

President Richard Nixon was in the White House dealing with the rumors that were arising in the aftermath of the Vietnam War and the publication of the Pentagon Papers. In a plush condominium called the Watergate along the Potomac River in downtown Washington, D.C., a scandal was about to erupt concerning the secret tapings of Nixon's opponents at the Democratic National Committee.

Within the walls of the News-Gazette, day-to-day life seemed normal. Marajen was keeping a close eye on the business and on Michael. Michael had been making numerous trips to Rome, which Marajen assumed were for business. But Michael wasn't traveling alone. One of the writers at the paper was having an affair with Michael. When Michael went to Italy, his mistress either went with him or was sent over shortly after his arrival. The love affair grew and continued until someone leaked the news to Marajen.

After finding incriminating letters, which she later kept in a locked drawer of her desk, Marajen went on a rampage and had the woman fired immediately. Marajen and Michael had a very vocal argument where Michael denied nothing. At home, Marajen threw some of Michael's possessions out of their house and told him to get out. The fights continued off and on for weeks. On one occasion in late March 1974, she called police about a suspicious noise outside of the house. When the police arrived, Michael came out of the bushes. After a physical confrontation with the police on the lawn, the Champaign police told him to find other accommodations that night. Marajen, learning that it was Michael, had had enough. She went upstairs and tossed his remaining clothes out a second story window.

Soon afterwards Marajen filed for an Order of Protection against Michael and then for divorce. The mistress, the former wife of a professor at the University of Illinois in Urbana, was informed by some authority at the paper to leave the job and town. There was some speculation that Marajen paid her the sum of $25,000 to leave town permanently. From Champaign, the mistress acquired a job in Indiana, but Marajen had her traced and contacted her employer with horrid stories of what she had done at the News-Gazette. Third-person rumors were not enough to terminate her, so Marajen paid the Indiana employer a large amount of money to guarantee her termination.

Michael stayed away from Champaign as much as possible, which wasn't hard with his contacts in Rome. All in all, Michael was happy it was over. He told insiders that Marajen was a controlling bitch with frequent mood changes. He retained Howard Baker as his attorney and only returned to Champaign to conduct business. First on the list of things to do was make a new will. Marajen had contacted her own attorney. Marajen and her attorney exchanged several phone calls over the course of many months concerning her divorce from Michael. It appeared as though the only way out would be an even split among the various properties and the money. This wasn't what Marajen had in mind. This wasn't the way it would be.

About a month after Marajen threw Michael out, a strange thing happened at the Chinigo house. A Chicago investigator and an FBI agent interviewed Marajen about Sam Giancana, the godfather of the Chicago crime family. Marajen's "no knowledge" answers to their questions proved no help to them. She acted very innocent when questioned and only admitted to knowing Rosselli from their acquaintance in Hollywood years before. Marajen stated further that she had no idea who Giancana was. This was a lie, but the FBI did not push the point. Did her ties with the Mob go deeper than Johnny Rosselli? Marajen knew Giancana was in Cuba at the same time that she was there on vacation. He and Phyllis McGuire were sitting very close to Marajen and her guests at the same nightclub. Marajen was introduced to both of them that evening. Did the FBI know that Rosselli had a lengthy visit with Marajen just before the assassination of President Kennedy?

The encounter with the FBI somewhat shook Marajen. When she notified Johnny, the contact between them was sporadic and very brief. Johnny had been spending most of his time in California rebuilding his position with "the boys." Marajen went about her normal routine but began to look over her shoulder.

Marajen, furious with Michael's affair and his wanting half of everything that she had built or inherited before he would agree to a divorce, placed a call to Bill Harvey, who was in Europe completing some work for Rosselli. She was hoping that Bill would side with her and possibly scare Michael with a threat. She all but screamed at Bill with what Michael had done to her and the embarrassment it was causing her in the community. She referred to the mistress as a "cleaning lady," knowing perfectly well that she was a writer. She told Harvey that Michael had no class, to leave her for a cleaning lady. Marajen was splenetic. She had assumed that Michael would crawl back, asking for forgiveness. But this didn't happen. When Johnny left Marajen, she thought he too would come back. The fact that Michael didn't bothered her more than the affair. Gazette employees said Michael had never been as happy as when he was away from Marajen. She was controlling and manipulative, and he was glad to be out from under her. He stated, "Most of Marajen's friends were homos and whores ... not his type of friends."

Feeling cast aside for another woman, Marajen made more phone calls to Bill Harvey. In one phone call, Marajen became intimately suggestive to Bill, but Bill was not willing to jeopardize his marriage for her.[31] When Bill showed no interest in her, she shifted gears and contacted Rosselli. Her vanity peaking, Marajen had a portrait of herself painted and sent to Johnny. The portrait was the bait to heat up a simmering romance, once again proving she could get anyone she wanted.

Using Bill Harvey to glean legal advice, Marajen invited the Harveys to her home for a weekend and invited them to dine with her and her friends at the Champaign Country Club. Bill and Marajen discussed what each party was expecting and whether Marajen would bend in any areas to get the divorce over with that much faster. Marajen wanted nothing to do with any of it. She told Bill that she would make headlines if she had to, to get rid of Michael. For several weeks Bill and Marajen exchanged phone calls concerning the pending divorce. She had been told straight out that it would not be simple and quick. There was too much at stake, and Michael wanted his cut. Marajen was not going to relent. He was getting nothing if she could prevent it. Bill told Marajen the facts and what he could do if she hired him for her counsel. He explained the divorce laws to her and about his conversations with Michael's attorney, Howard Baker. Marajen was outraged. Bill Harvey wasn't going to play dirty. After fuming a few days, Marajen called Johnny. Rosselli had been released from prison less than a year and was enjoying peace in his life. Even the various agencies that had dogged him for three decades weren't on his heels. He was not able to talk to her at the time, so Marajen left a message for Johnny to return her call soon.

Late one summer evening in July 1974, the phone rang at the Chinigo home. Marajen took the call. After typical small talk and some laughter Marajen spoke of her wish. There was a pause, and then Marajen made a seething comment: "You owe me!" The caller was Rosselli, and it is assumed he may not have wanted to be a party to this demand until Marajen reminded him of the $50,000 she had given him some time back. There was more hushed conversation, and then Marajen said into the phone, "I thought you would see it my way." Then the phone went dead. Two days later Marajen received a call from Rosselli.

Rosselli found an excuse to return to Rome several days later under an assumed name. He still had not obtained U.S. citizenship. The government, not totally forgetting about Rosselli, still looked for any way to have him deported. In Rome he met with Bill Harvey. This may have been part of Rosselli's cover should the various agencies be watching him in Rome. Around midnight August 13, Michael Chinigo was observed walking with a friend on a Rome street. Suddenly shots rang out in the silence of night. Both Michael and his friend fell to the ground. Eventually, Rome police arrived, and minutes after that the police summoned an ambulance, which transported Michael to the San Giovanni Hospital. The friend that Michael was walking with supposedly remained in the street. Nothing was mentioned as to his condition. Did he die or recover, and how was he injured? There were two shots. Two shots were fired to kill Michael; did one hit him and the other his friend? These questions have never been answered. The police reports and the media coverage stated that Michael took the gun his friend was carrying and shot himself. These were not the true circumstances. Michael did not attempt suicide. Instead …a debt was paid.[32]

In Champaign, midnight Illinois time, after the attempted murder of Michael Chicago, Marajen was awakened by a phone call, a short call that said, "It is done." Marajen replaced the phone receiver and returned to bed. The call was placed from Miami by a friend of Rosselli, who remained in Rome after the shooting. Later that day she received another phone call from Rome. This call was from employees at the villa, giving her the known details of the shooting. She was also told that Michael survived the shooting. Marajen acted very much like the shaken wife over the phone but returned to her daily work when the conversation was over. The only out of the ordinary thing she did was place pictures of Michael in several places in her bedroom. This was something she had never done before. For weeks after the affair was out, Michael's name was never mentioned. But now, to Marajen's employees she seemed nervous. She was constantly agitated and short with them. Why? Marjen had a problem …the job was not over.

On August 15th or 16th Bill Harvey and Johnny Rosselli arrived in Champaign and spoke with Marajen. The stay was short and business-like. The conversation was not fully overheard by anyone in her house, except for, "It will be taken care of," by Johnny and Marajen's response: "Good." It is believed that following this brief encounter Rosselli left for the West Coast and Harvey went back home to Indianapolis.

Marajen was not the same for several days. She avoided friends and social contacts and from that day forward insisted on having a light on in her bedroom at all times. She was cruel to her loyal employees and any guests in her home. According to a very close friend, Marajen feared that Michael would send someone to do her harm or, once recovered, he would return himself. She hired a team of six security people to cover her twenty-four hours a day.

In the Rome hospital Michael wanted to speak to Marajen,

and at no time did he pass blame for the incident on her. Marjen didn't believe him, and his words only increased her fear that he had put a contract out on her. Michael did tell her that he would contact the IRS about some jewelry that she had imported illegally. This frightened Marajen even further and heightened her fear that he would put a contract out on her. With this fear and because he was in Rome and she was in the States, she made arrangements for a Bruno Bacci (further unidentified) to secure the villa. Michael's mistress, hearing of the shooting, flew to Rome and made several attempts to see Michael, but when she got to the hospital she was told that he had been moved somewhere else. This cat and mouse game continued for some time. When the mistress arrived at the hospital that Michael had been moved to, she learned that he had been moved again. Whether Michael had, indeed, been moved or if the mistress was just told that is unclear. But the mistress did not see Michael.

Further interviews indicated that Michael underwent surgery once or twice in the following five to six weeks, but the doctors were unable to save him. On October 11, 1974, Michael was pronounced dead. The interesting fact here is that just days after the shooting, Michael was walking around the hospital with his mind intact. Then surgery, possible two, was performed, and subsequently he died. It should be remembered that on the day that Bill Harvey and Johnny Rosselli came to visit Marajen after the news was out about the shooting, the one phrase that was clearly said by Rosselli was "It will be taken care of," followed by "Good" from Marajen. Was the surgery ordered by someone? Was someone sent in to finish the job? Was someone paid to make it appear that surgery was needed, which then proved unsuccessful? These questions remain unanswered. Sources in Italy refused to speculate over the phone. Silence, and then the subject was dropped.

Controversy also lingered over the status of the friend that Michael was with the night of the attempted assassination. The official police reports stated that the friend was also shot and remained in a coma. There was never a follow-up report about the friend as to whether he ever gained consciousness or he died. The report only stated that Michael had taken the friend's gun and shot himself. The report stated that Michael was sent for emergency treatment. There was no mention of the friend he was supposedly with. Questions remain: Was there someone else walking with him that night? Or was someone paid to say Michael was with someone?

Marajen learned after his death that in his will Michael had left everything, minus his share of the villa, to his mistress. His part of the villa was to go to the American government as a retreat for journalists. The United States government didn't want it, nor, as it turns out, did the Italian government. Michael had also made monetary provisions for his mistress in his will to include the mention of the emerald ring he had given her years before. But when the will was read, there was no mention of such provisions. Did Marajen secretly have Michael's will changed? One thing that Marajen could not change was the fact that Michael was buried in Rome next to his first wife, Gisenne.

In mid-October 1974, Johnny Rosselli visited Marajen's villa, Torre di Civiat. At the close of the visit he wrote in the guest book, "New Page, new Life, Affectionately, John." No further correspondence was given. This was an obscure, cryptic message to Marajen that the deed was complete. She had no further need to be afraid of him.

# Look Into My Crystal Ball

The Oxford Dictionary defines palmistry as "the art of telling a person's character by examining the lines and configuration of the palm." It is also referred to as chiromancy, meaning prophecy, or the foretelling of events, by the lines of the hand. Palmistry has been used for centuries, and the Greek civilization can be credited for the study of the hands. Even the Bible makes reference to it, in the original Hebrew form of the Book of Job, with the passage: "God caused the signs or seals on the hands of all men that the sons of men might know their work."

People in general have always been curious to understand the miracle of knowledge between the present and the future. It is common now to say "ESP" in most circles. This covers the field in a general way for those who have not seriously studied the paranormal or clairvoyance.

One person who demonstrated her physic abilities was Greta Alexander of Delavan, Illinois. Greta didn't always have the talent, and hers arrived in an unusual way. In April of 1961, Greta, eight months pregnant, was trying to sleep during a storm. While lying in bed, she watched lightning dance between the slats of the new Venetian blinds she had hung earlier in the day. Thunder and lightening dominated the hours, and all she could do was watch. Suddenly a bolt of lightning struck her house. The window came out of its casing, and the Venetian blind was wrapped around her body. Worse yet, the bed was on fire! By the time the fire trucks arrived, the house was consumed in smoke, and the entire family was standing out in the street. Several hours later the fire department had the fire out and the bedroom window boarded up, and the Alexander family was back in their home, huddled together, sleeping in the living room. Greta, concerned about the unborn baby, went to Peoria the next morning to be checked. Her doctor assured her she and the baby were fine.

Shortly after the baby's birth, Greta began to notice different things about herself. She was seeing visions. She knew ahead of time when the phone was going to ring. She knew ahead of time when someone was going to show up at her house. She began to study books and other material that explained what was going on. She kept her psychic ability a secret and considered it a gift. Feeling that the gift was sent from God, Greta was determined to use it to help people in any way she could.

A few years later Greta was referred to as a parapsychologist. She was a popular lecturer, consultant, and author for more than twenty years. She even served as consultant for the movie Sixth Sense. Greta was called upon by roughly five hundred police agencies across the nation to work on cases involving murder, missing persons, thefts, and arson investigations. Her success-to-failure ratio all depends on who you talk to. Some say she was overrated, and others say that case after case was solved because of the pictures she saw in her mind. She had a palm reading clientele that stretched to the borders of America. She "read" for Ted Pugh, Carrie Fisher, Ruth Warrick (of the All My Children soap opera), Debbie Reynolds, and Marajen Stevick Chinigo.[33]

Though brought up in a deeply religious family, Marajen dabbled in the world of the paranormal. She had visited Greta several times over the years, but the date Michael was to be shot Marajen made a rush trip to Delevan. On the way there

Marajen seemed agitated and troubled. She squirmed in the car seat and stared out the window most of the trip. Marajen's session with Greta was brief and troubling for both women. On the way home she was very emotional, succumbing to brief bouts of tears. Greta had told Marajen that something terrible would happen to someone very close to her very soon.

Prior to her scheduled appointment with Greta, Marajen had talked with a priest for a great length of time, and she made several long-distance phone calls, trying to reach Johnny. There seemed to be no answer on the other end of the phone. Not making contact with Johnny, Marajen became extremely troubled by something. She cancelled her scheduled meetings and continued trying to contact Johnny. When that failed, she called friends in Italy in hopes they had seen him or could reach him. Did she have second thoughts about wanting Michael eliminated? Did she want to renege on the order but found it was too late to stop it? We will never know. She never shared her fears with her friends, not even the close ones.

# Life Goes On

Grieving for a long period of time and wearing black were not in the style of either Scarlett O'Hara or Marajen Chinigo. She soon succeeded in clearing her mind and moving on. With money she acquired with the sale of the television station, she made plans to return to Palm Springs, California. There she spotted a home in the wealthy suburb of Thunderbird Heights. In a matter of days she was the owner of a house. Marjen could start over. She could put the past behind her and leave it buried. In Palm Springs she would be surrounded by movie stars, wealthy businesspeople, and even a president.

Marajen quickly had some of her antique European furniture sent from Italy to her new home in Palm Springs. It is said that most of furnishings were not typical of California décor, and many were imitations of true antiques—some not very good imitations. Neighbors joked that her home was like a museum of odd pieces atypical of the California highlife style. This didn't bother Marajen. She loved them and wanted the furnishings in her new home. Her early days in Thunderbird Heights were filled with work that had to be done, which included employing a housekeeper on a full-time basis. On the neighbors' advice, she employed a gardener who was well respected in the neighborhood. She shopped for a dressmaker, silversmith, and massage therapist. Once the basics were handled, Marajen was comfortable returning to Champaign to take care of management issues at the paper.

A month later Marajen was preparing for her return to Palm Springs and her first party in her new home. Her housekeeper, Elvira Hernandez, was to prepare the house to Marajen's specifications and have a choice of menus prepared for Marajen's approval. The guest list was made and approved by Marajen over the phone long before invitations were sent out. On the day that she was to leave Champaign, Marajen planned to gather coolers of steaks to take with her. She would tell her guests in California that the steaks were "authentic Illinois corn-fed Angus steaks." Her personal secretary in Champaign had packed her luggage and made the final arrangements for her departure. Usually, on these trips Marajen's personal secretary was part of the entourage that went to California.

A story goes that at Marajen's introduction party, Alice Faye, the 1930s pin-up icon and invited guest, arrived in a taxi and requested that the driver stay at the Chinigo home with the engine and meter running just in case the party was a bust. It wasn't, and Alice stayed two hours; all while the cab's meter was running.[34] Among others guests were actors Larry Storch and Dennis James. Her special guests were Ed and Chevy Foster, owners and publishers of Celebrity-Society. This was the magazine Marajen wished to be seen in; it was the who's who magazine for California.

She spared no entertainment expenses. Her food menu would include such foods as sautéed gras caviar with trimmings and champagne, to impress her list of elite guests. Though not a star herself, she made a point of knowing all the right people and having them attend. Frank Sinatra was always on the guest list, and he attended a couple of times but started refusing when she asked him to sing. Frank graciously tried to tell her that he attended her parties to relax, not to entertain. No matter to Marajen. She loved the glamour his presence projected, and that was all that mattered to her. Mrs. Joe Wambaugh remembers the lavish parties Marajen hosted. She referred to Marajen as a strikingly attractive lady and extremely charming. Mrs. Wambaugh was infatuated with Marajen's artwork and said Marajen always put beautiful, personal touches to things that set her parties apart from others. [35] Zsa Zsa Gabor attended several of Marajen's parties, as did former President and First Lady Gerald Ford. On two occasions Johnny Rosselli was there.

Lisa Figus, an actress on the soap opera General Hospital, whose first husband played the character Larry Tate on Bewitched, spoke of Marajen's friends in California as people who only wanted something from her. Lisa liked Marajen very much and enjoyed her wit and charm. But Lisa could see through the glitz and saw that Marajen seemed so naïve and gullible. People used her. Outside of her artistic talents for painting and hosting beautiful parties, she had nothing to offer them. One of Marajen's closer friends in California was Dena Ivancie, who found Marajen "a charming individual. She could be quite funny and could entertain out of this world." [36]

If not entertaining in Palm Springs, Marajen entertained at her Italian villa. Each year she invited a few of her Champaign friends to enjoy a few days at the villa. In preparing for her elaborate parties, Marajen would be driven to Bologna, which offered her Italy's culinary favorites. Should she meet close friends from Italy while shopping, she would call the housekeeper at the villa to add the friends' names to the guest list. One such friend was Professor Michele Ingenito of Italy. The remarkably romantic man stated he "adored Marajen." He met Marajen in the early 1990s. Initially he thought she was president of a prestigious American university. Marajen never corrected him—a case where Marajen enriched the truth to make the rich and famous accept her. (37) Mr. Ingenito was infatuated with Marajen and found her little deceit excusable. He even wrote a novel with Marajen as one of the main characters.

Her parties at the villa were the subject of both gossip columns and her neighbors in Ravello for days. For shock value, Marajen would have nude men and women lying around her pool when guests arrive. She found enjoyment in having gay boys around, and if drugs helped to loosen them up, entirely the better. She enjoyed the company of notable people, and those with titles, like herself, pleased her even more. With them, Marajen felt she was in the company of people on her level.

Occasionally Marajen displayed her two personalities for unsuspecting people. Marajen's pleasant, warm, and friendly side was displayed at her villa one autumn. She was preparing a luncheon for the Queen of the Netherlands. Marajen was in the kitchen helping her housekeeper, Anna Maria, prepare the meal, when the queen showed up an hour earlier than Marajen expected. Marajen, hair in rollers and dressed in a housecoat, invited her in, took her to the kitchen, and pulled out a chair for her to sit in. The two women chatted like old friends until the food was ready. The queen spoke of Marajen's warmth and ability to make someone feel comfortable in an unsuspecting way.

Another story shows the other Marajen. Jackie Onassis was invited to the villa for lunch when Marajen learned she would be sailing from Greece to Italy. A scheduling mishap put Jackie O at Marajen's door a day early. Marajen opened the door, bitterly informed her that she was a day early, and slammed the door in her face. Rarely did Marajen make concessions when others were at fault, but she expected many when she was in error.

Marajen's closest neighbor at the villa was author and playwright Gore Vidal, whose villa, like Marajen's, was perched high above the Amalfi coast line. Gore was most often seen in the company of political and socially notable people. That he was related to Jackie Kennedy through one of his mother's marriages also enticed Marajen to pursue a relationship with the man. Marajen and Gore were known to have heated political discussions, as Gore was a Democrat at the time and Marajen a devoted Republican. But Gore eventually found Marajen "shallow and a bore." Hoping time would change Gore's opinion of her, and in hopes of keeping him as a potential guest for future parties, Marajen once sent a personal invitation with her driver for an upcoming celebration. When the driver returned, Marajen asked what his response was. The driver stated that he didn't give a response. Marajen, puzzled, asked what Gore did. The driver said that he slammed the door in his face. Marajen's comment was, "That must be a no." From then on Marajen referred to Gore Vidal as the man she hated. Marajen would say she formed her opinion due to their very different political beliefs.

On a cruise, Marajen met Rudy Percoco. A wealthy man, Percoco owned a yacht and often visited North America. The two of them had an off-and-on affair for a few years when Percoco was in Italy. He would stop at the villa for an afternoon and then return to his fortress. Rudy eventually told Marajen that he was married. Seeing no future for her, Marajen became bored with the arrangement and severed the relationship.

# Thunder in the Distance

If the name John Hirschfeld is mentioned to older residents in Champaign, a chuckle will precede the remark, "Ah, yes, the golden boy," followed by a lowered head and a shake or two. John Hirschfeld's life personified the American dream, and he was the golden boy in Champaign for almost three decades.

Growing up a farm boy in Champaign County, John had humble and honest roots. He started his road to success as a paper carrier for the News-Gazette; the Chinigo house was on his route. At Christmastime, Marajen and Michael would have hot cocoa and cookies prepared for delivery people during the holiday. When John delivered the paper one evening, Marajen invited him in for the warm snack. In the room where John sat, a wind-up music box sat on the piano and played a tune that enthralled him. In later years John would say that if he wanted anything that was Marajen's, it would have been that music box. (38)

After graduating from Notre Dame University and Notre Dame Law School, he served in the Illinois state legislature for six years in the 1970s, and he was a partner in a noted law firm in Champaign. In the 1980s he was chairman of the Republican Party in Champaign.

Marajen and Michael watched John grow up, and Marajen

considered him the child she never had. She catered to his every whim. His association, as a lawyer for the paper, with Michael was professional while Michael was in charge. After Michael died John began to push for more authority, and Marajen, wishing for someone to handle the reins, was all too happy to have John take over. Marajen, who was rarely in town to oversee the paper and who didn't really care about the journalistic side of the business, was eager to allow Hirshfeld the responsibility so that she could resume her life of parties and travels. Liking his intelligence and charm, Marajen made him president and CEO of the News Gazette, the Tolono County Star, and radio stations WHMS FM and WDWS AM in the late '80s. About the same time, Hirshfeld launched his own Rush Limbaugh-type political radio talk show. Not pleased with any of her previous attorneys, Maraajen also made John Hirschfeld her personal attorney. This, of course, proved to be a conflict of interest and led to double-dipping in Marajen's income.

John's convincing ways won him the confidence of the community. He stressed family values in lectures and invited speeches throughout the country. But many stated that John, too, had two sides, and those who thought they knew him, didn't. He was very different at work than he was at home.

Pleased with Hirshfeld's work at the News-Gazette, Marajen extended John's duties across the big pond to Italy. John was to oversee Torre de Civita when legal matters arose and supervise the employees, both the villa's household staff and the farmers who rented land from her. John also attended parties at the villa but rarely, if ever, with his wife. Former employees of the newspaper said John always came by himself.

Rita, John's first wife, a beautiful Southern belle, met John in law school during the 1960s. After their marriage, John's relatives never made her feel like she was part of the family, and neither did Marajen Chinigo. Rita stated that she never received one phone call from Marajen over the years John was under her employ. She was also excluded from social events involving the

News-Gazette and any personal parties that Marajen hosted. John didn't want her involved in his work or the social life that came with his position. During the thirty years they were married, John impressed upon her that her place was in the home caring for the children. She came into the family and marriage naïve, and John wanted her to remain naïve. (39)

Hirshfeld, always in demand for county, state, and national committees, shocked many News-Gazette readers shortly after his appointment to a national education panel when he wrote an article in support of David Duke, the former Ku Klux Klan leader. A former panel member was rumored to say that even he had to read the article twice to see the point John was trying to make. Duke was running for president on the Republican ticket, and Hirschfeld liked Duke's points on illegal immigration and higher taxes. That was why John supported him.

John carried the ticket to fame and fortune, but something happened. His drinking became heavier and heavier, and greed stepped in. He told close associates that he dealt with Marajen's moods by drinking. Though she financed a few vacations for John and his family, she was normally very hard on her employees. She would greet them with a smile and act as though they were important, but she really didn't care about their lives. Marajen was not at the paper on a daily basis, and the responsibility for running all of her businesses, plus the villa, possibly caused John to think his salary wasn't enough. He was overloaded with responsibility, and Marajen would not let him delegate to other staff members. He was experiencing absolute power, and he wanted compensation for same. But absolute power corrupts.

Marajen was spending money faster than it came in. She had to keep inventing ways to entice her friends to visit her in Italy. Her trips on the Concorde with a select group weren't cheap. Money seemed of no concern to her. But the purse was going dry. She had purchased a yacht she had in Florida years earlier and had not paid the taxes on it. The IRS, through an audit, confiscated the yacht for back taxes, and a year before John Hirschfeld was dismissed, she became angry when he told her she couldn't have the private jet she wanted because there wasn't enough money. "I can't just fly in a jet that anyone else flies in!" she said, trying to justify her need for it. Marajen was still trying to stay on top.

On two different occasions, accountants for the newspaper noticed things didn't look right and approached Marajen with the proof. Marajen took the problem to John, and he turned it around. That very day the accountant who had showed her the discrepancy in the books was fired. The second accountant didn't fare any better and received the same verdict.

John drank more heavily than ever. His excessive drinking brought out Marajen's compassion; she made arrangements for him to be registered in a rehab center in Indiana. How long John stayed is unclear, but one day he just left. No dismissal no signing out, he just left. In 1996 Marajen paid for John's entrance fee to the Bob Hope Golf Classic, to the tune of $4,500 in hopes of straightening him out. But the underlying reason was to cozy up to another famous star. A few weeks after the golf classic, John began to change. He began having affairs. When Marajen found out she confronted him, and she believed his denials. But the shocking and bitter truth came when John took a woman to Marajen's home in California. It wasn't Mrs. Hirshfeld.(40) Was the shiny gold cloud around John evaporating? Was his human side surfacing?

People who worked with both John Hirschfeld and Marajen believed Marajen tried to work with John. She was concerned about his drinking and his family. Most feel John's major decline from Marjen's graces grew when his marriage took a drastic spiral downward. At least that's the reason Marajen would give when questioned about him. This was probably the problem she could deal with publicly, rather than admit to what he was doing to her financially. Dramatizing his infidelities seemed atypical for Marajen, with her various sexual shenanigans and rendezvous in and out of marriage. But John stood out in her businesses, and he represented her, so he had to be perfect.

By early fall of 1997, Marajen had made the decision to terminate John. Once again she had been hurt by someone she trusted, and revenge became the next order of business. None of the attorneys she contacted over the matter gave her any satisfaction. Some even refused to tackle the job. So Marajen looked deeper. She requested the same kind of help Rosselli had given her. A close friend of Marajen's was asked to contact the individual of Marajen's choice—a "hit man," a person who, for a price, could make life easier for someone else. This is what Marajen was looking for in response for what John Hirshfeld had done to her. But the friend refused to do it. So she took on the task the legal way. She needed someone who was top shelf, with lots of crescendo. John Trutter of Rancho Mirage, California, retained one of the best in the legal field: Don Reuben.

Marajen had used the services of several attorneys over the years, but none were quite as colorful as Don Reuben, the former attorney for the Chicago Tribune, the Chicago Bears football team, NBC and ABC television networks, and the Catholic Archdiocese of Chicago, the largest in the United States. Reuben's specialty was advising clients regarding internal affairs and take-over threats. The winning side of the chart for court cases won by the Chicago Tribune is an example of how their cases were handled. The son of a Chicago mobster, Reuben had his name changed to conceal his relationship to the Mob. The Chicago Tribune hired him as their negotiator in business dealings and court cases. It is said that Reuben could convince a judge to rule in favor of the Tribune by simply dropping a few names, dates, and places, using dossiers the paper, until recently, kept on state and federal judges just for this purpose.

Mr. Rueben also lived in Thunderbird Heights, California, and had heard of Marajen Chinigo. Marajen began the depressing job of terminating John Hirshfeld. She phoned her villa from her Champaign residence and announced her plans to dethrone John Hirshfeld, saying he would no longer hurt her or anyone else.

After a few phone conversations and a retainer, Reuben and his team arrived in Champaign and went to work. Together Marajen and the team of attorneys went over the books and quickly concluded that John Hirschfeld was in trouble. The CEO and corporate attorney for the News-Gazette had been double-dipping to an amount of over one million dollars. Marajen agreed to sue for the purpose of recovering what funds the paper could. To add fuel to the fire, Reuben also reported Hirshfeld's actions to the Attorney Registration and Disciplinary Committee of the Illinois Supreme Court, better known as the ARDC. Once their investigation was complete, the compiled figures led to the ruin of John.

Marajen had paid John Hirshfeld an annual salary of $290,000 in 1993. By 1996 it had grown to $360,000 a year. Apparently not enough to live on, even with travel expenses paid on top of the salary, John started double-billing her for legal services. In his last year of employment, he was drawing slightly over $400,000. Marajen felt the legal services Hirshfeld provided her with were part of his annual salary. She assumed that the legal fees he charged her for were actually part of his salary as CEO of the paper. Either John thought differently, or he attempted to prepare the billing to look otherwise. Another sin Hirshfeld committed was telling yarns while giving tours to guests at the villa. He often told stories that involved client confidences, and he told them without the authority to do so. The only part of this disclosure that ruffled Marajen's feathers was when John mentioned the fact that she was divorced.

Hirshfeld and his attorney, Mr. Gair, tried plea bargaining with the ARDC With such a serious matter at stake, John threw in a proposal. He offered to bomb Yugoslavia if the embezzling allegations were dropped! To avoid a trial that would make details public, John pled guilty to excessively overbilling Marajen Chinigo by 1.78 million dollars, directing an employee to improperly notarize a certificate in connection with a deed, and using a client's signature stamp without authority. His license was suspended for at least one year. At home John was served with divorce papers; the knife in the heart came when his children all sided with their mother. John's life was in shreds.

When speaking to her close friends in Italy, Marajen changed her opinion of John. There was a time when John was her right-hand person, the man who had all the answers, someone she had taken under her wing and relied on to run her business when she was not able to do so. She treated his family as hers, minus Rita, and lavished expensive vacations and gifts on them. Now, John had taken advantage of her and used her for his own personal benefit. Marajen had put John in the wonderful position he held at the paper. Because of her, he held a much respected place in the community. He was an intelligent man with charm and charisma. His law practice dealt primarily with pro bono work in the field of adoption, and he often wrote controversial articles that were published in notable journals. Now his kingdom was toppling, and Marajen Chinigo was totally disenchanted with him.

On the assumption that the worse was legally over, Marajen called Rueben's office. Reuben informed Marajen that John was very polite but was concerned about his law firm. To save face Rueben told John to save face and resign from the firm for personal reasons.

Rueben continued to tell Marajen some of the other things John had done that she wasn't aware of, such as placing all of her charities in a trust to last for a hundred years, without knowing whether the charity would even be around for a hundred years. Reuben would have that document corrected. In 1980 John had a trust written up to oversee Marajen's various businesses should she die, at a cost of 1 million a year, with himself named as the recipient of the million dollars.

As soon as she concluded the phone conversation with Reuben, Marajen called Anna Maria at her villa in Italy. "The monkey is off my back now ...he is off everyone's back. He has mental problems, and I can't help him. I thought he had done many good things for the paper and me, but now I see that he was only covering for himself. Mr. Reuben is sending four lawyers down to Champaign to go through John's stuff. John won't be allowed in the museum in the basement of the Gazette. It's over, Anna Maria ...thank God, it is over, Oh; do you know what John did? He had already sent out letters to people about selling the newspaper! Maybe by some miracle he will see that people really cared for him, but he has to help himself!"(41)

By mid-afternoon the same day, Don Reuben had a prepared statement to be read to the employees at the News-Gazette regarding Hirshfeld's status with the News-Gazette.

# Some Things Never Change

Once John Hirshfeld was out of her life, Marajen again planned parties, and life returned to normal. Her life centered on entertaining. Some were successful; others were not. She had prearranged a showing for her art work in Peoria, Illinois. A bus was chartered to take her and some chosen friends to view it. By the time the bus got to Peoria, most people on board were drunk and never got to see the art. In fact, they were not even allowed to enter the facility. Those times were rare but memorable. On December 5, 1997, her paintings were shown at Krannert Center at the University of Illinois. Her work was entitled A Lifetime of Beauty. Marajen continued to look for ways to keep her name prominent, struggling to the end to get her name in lights.

She bestowed monetary gifts for causes that would reflect notice on her. She promised Oral Roberts a million dollars for a center at the Oral Roberts University. When Oral's son appeared at her door to collect the check, Marajen invited him in. He stated several times that he couldn't stay; once the check was in his hands he immediately left, returning to Willard airport to fly home. This was a slap in Marajen's face, and early the next day she stopped payment on the check. A suit was initiated, and Marajen finally forked over the funds, with a very brusque note attached. It was apparent to Marajen that Oral Roberts wasn't interested in Marajen's wish to promote journalism; he simply wanted the money. Today her name is on the graduate center at Oral Roberts University for which the donation was slated.

Marajen was slowly learning that it wasn't her name or what she stood for that mattered. It was her money. People she thought were friends actually were not. Actor Richard and Francesca Harrison in California and Barbara Main in Champaign were probably the closest friends Marajen had. She continued to weave a network of stars that she called her friends, if only in her mind. When Bob Hope was starring at the Assembly Hall in Champaign, Marajen would insist on meeting with him at the Brass Rail restaurant. Marajen was always late, which irritated Hope. Employees at the restaurant stated that, Hope even referred to Marajen as a female dog in his aggravation over her lateness, Hope even referred to Marajen as a female dog. "I am her guest. She should be greeting me here!"

She was infatuated with Guy Lombardo, the famous band leader of the 1930s. She opened her home to him when he was performing in Champaign. She loved his music and the man and didn't hide her affection for him.

In the late 1990s the Chicago Tribune sent an emissary to meet with Marajen at her Champaign residence. The emissary's mission was to offer to purchase the News-Gazette. The Tribune's representative explained that one of her employees at the paper suggested her interest in selling the paper. This infuriated Marajen, though she remained calmed until he left. If Marajen suspected who the employee was, she did not let on to anyone.

Her interest in the newspaper became minimal as the years progressed. Occasionally she would contact John Foreman, who reigns as current editor and publisher, about a specific article she didn't approve of or her preference for a picture that she felt should be printed. Otherwise, she made no effort to stay personally involved in the business of the paper. Once or twice a year she would appear and shake hands with old timers and then sit in an ornate chair placed on a raised platform and request that her employees walk by and kiss her hand. She might be old, but she was still Countess Marajen Chinigo.

Marajen never gave up her search for fame and recognition. It wasn't enough to have her name on invitations to elite functions or registers. She felt it had to be secured with money. She wanted the spotlight to forever shine on her; too late in life did she realize it was really only her money that people and groups wanted. She did donate generously to the Champaign County Humane Society, probably because of her fondness for dogs, especially her beloved poodle Popcorn. She made a healthy $5,000 donation to the Bush-Cheney campaign in the 2002 to 2003 fiscal year, which netted her an official letter of thanks from Washington. Marajen supported the University of Illinois throughout her life in Champaign. She made a hefty donation of one million dollars to the College of Applied Life Sciences at the University of Illinois in Urbana.

In her never-ending search for ways to keep her name in the headlines, Marajen discovered that by contributing $10,000 to $24,000 to the University of Alabama in Birmingham she would become an ambassador at the college. This was done but little fanfare followed. She built a senior citizen's home in California and helped to fund a hospital in Rancho Mirage. But most of her smaller charities received only modest donations.

# The Final Secrets

In the spring of 1975, the Senate Intelligence Committee heard a series of special hearings involving several members of organized crime. During June 1975, Johnny Rosselli testified before the committee. Rosselli's testimony was supposed to establish a link between organized crime and the CIA in the assassination plots against Castro and, ultimately, the John F. Kennedy assassination. On two different occasions Rosselli was summoned to appear and answer questions before a special group on the committee. Initially he kept his usually quite short responses direct. The only admission the suave and debonair Rosselli made was that he and Giancana were asked to plan a plot against Castro. He never said who asked him and never admitted to participating. When asked if he knew Judith Exner, he admitted that he did; during the period she was a girlfriend of Sam Giancana. Believing that Exner was the informant to President Kennedy about the CIA's plots to eliminate Castro, the Senate committee tried to weasel out a confession of the same from Rosselli. No admission from Rosselli came. In one testimony he reflected back on a business trip to Illinois to see a girlfriend who owned a newspaper. He, of course, was referring to Marajen Chinigo. He did not elaborate, except to say they had been friends for years.

Rosselli's boss, Chicago's crime boss Sam Giancana, was also slated to give testimony, but he never made it to court. During a night in June 1975, in his basement apartment, Sam Giancana was gunned down while he made a late night snack. Had Johnny Rosselli conspired with Sam Trafficante to have Giancana wacked? It is certainly possible; Rosselli feared the old Don would crumble under examination. Giancana was unhappy with the seemingly close friendship that Rosselli and Tranfficante had. Rosselli had made it known ever since the Castro plots that he wanted to move up in the ranks. He was gambling on which crime family to stick with. He had to decide which family was stronger. Was Rosselli simply eliminating the competition? Giancana's demise may have come anyway, but with the Senate hearings, the time was ripe to do the deed now.

After a third testimony before the Church committee, Rosselli returned to his sister's home in Plantation, Florida. While there he contacted his friend Byrnie Foy in Los Angeles to pitch a movie idea. Foy, a movie producer heard Rosselli's pitch, which involved a gangster helping the U.S. government kill Castro, but the plan explodes. At the same time Castro's men were plotting to kill the seated president of the United States. Foy brushed the idea off, believing it wouldn't sell. A short time later, in May, Rosselli met up with friend Jimmy Fratianno to again push the movie idea and perhaps seek funds to finance the film. On this visit, Jimmy cautioned Johnny to watch himself. Jimmy had heard that Trafficante feared Rosselli had set him up during the hearings and that the government was on his trail.

By July 1976, word was leaking out from other Mafia members that Rosselli had better watch his back. Johnny quipped to his attorney and others, "Stop worrying about me. I'm not afraid to die." On July 28, 1976, his attorney made a final plea to Johnny by phone to leave Miami. Again, he refused, because he didn't feel threatened. Sometime after that phone call, he told his sister that he was going to go play golf. He never returned home. His 1975 Chevrolet was found parked at the Miami International Airport with the golf clubs in the trunk, where Johnny had put them. Law enforcement agencies felt that Johnny had skipped the country. Maybe he had taken the advice and gone to Mexico or some island.

After a couple of weeks, Johnny's body was found by two fishermen off Biscayne Bay near Miami, not far from long-ago cohort Curly Humphreys' home. Johnny had probably been suffocated; his body was cut in several pieces and put in an old fifty-five gallon drum. The drum had had holes punched in it and was wrapped in chains to ensure it would sink. But Johnny had the last word. As his body decomposed, gases formed that caused the drum to surface.

It is reasonable to think that the same people Rosselli worked with during his criminal career completed the death order. Had Johnny already talked too much, or would he have said too much if he testified again? If so, who would have placed the order? Probably it was Santo Trafficante, or maybe it was the CIA. Each had secrets of their own that they didn't want revealed. Johnny lived with the secrets and he died with the secrets.

Rosselli wasn't accorded the state funeral so many of his kind had received: no long, black limousines bearing wreaths of gaudy flowers, no throngs of people mourning on the street curbs for the loss of a man they loved. There were no eulogies about his contribution to the neighborhood or his patriotic efforts to help keep communism out of America, even if his ethical conscience was distorted. Johnny's funeral was very simple and attended by only a few family members. Then it was over, or as Johnny would have said, finito.

In 1985 Marajen Chinigo received the Outstanding Business Leader award. It was said this was probably the award that she really treasured. Other honors bestowed upon her over the years included life member of the President's Council of the University of Illinois and serving on the Foundation board of directors at the University. She was also a trustee of the Lincoln Academy. Her philanthropy began the Helen Mary Stevick Senior Citizens Center in her hometown of Champaign. She donated large sums to the National Academy of Arts and the University of Illinois Alpha Gamma Delta and Zonta International.

At Marajen's ninetieth birthday party, old friends gathered to honor the elderly countess. Even neighbors from her old California neighborhood Thunderbird Heights responded to the party invitation. One such person was Peter Marshall, former host of the television show Hollywood Squares, who came with his new love. When he arrived, Marajen answered the door bell and gave Peter a hug. Introduced to Peter's young, blond female companion dressed in a very low-cut blouse, Marajen said, "My dear, you look like a street walker!" That was the Marajen everyone had experienced at some point in their relationships with her. She was determined, pious, vibrant, sexy, romantic, compassionate, cold, and deadly lethal when she wanted to be.

One of Marajen's last house companions was Lisa Birch, who acquired her position with the aged dame when Marajen saw her working in Marajen's glorious flower beds. Lisa struck up a conversation with her, and as Lisa said, "The rest is history." By the time Lisa entered Marajen's life, she didn't travel much and spent most of her time within the confines of her large home in Champaign. The house consisted of many small rooms, which Marajen enlarged with mirrors everywhere. A gallery displayed photographs of the people who had entered Marajen's life over the course of her ninety years. It had an indoor swimming pool, where Marajen practiced water aerobics on a daily basis. Lisa found Marajen to be a very sweet person in her old age. She still maintained a sense of humor and was very kind and considerate to Lisa. The cold, hard lady who had ran a newspaper and traveled the world, making as many enemies as friends along the way, was now the elusive lady who kept to herself in her home. She had major health problems, which required bed rest.

In mid-December 2002, Marajen was hospitalized with blood clots in her legs. One clot went to her brain. On December 22, 2002, Marajen Stevick Chinigo's life drew to a close.

The dream that David Stevick gave life to and Marajen cultivated will probably continue for decades to come. The newspaper continues to grow and hopefully will remain independently owned and focused on being a community enterprise. It is hoped that the new administration will continue to share the vision for the future that all of the Stevick's did.

Since John Hirshfeld's departure and Marajen's death, there has been a natural shift in rank and positions. Sadly, after Marajen's death a few good, faithful employees at the residence and the paper were terminated immediately. One such person tried to draw unemployment following the termination, which was fought by the administration. Others were dismissed on trumped-up charges, with little or no proof or explanation. That can not be blamed on Marajen. There remains a strange web of secrecy about Marajen to this day. People who worked for her either at the newspaper or within her personal employ maintain their code of silence when Marajen' name is mentioned. And so the last of the secrets remain just that.

She often lived in a magical world among the beauty of life, flowers, and nature that she loved so much. The colors in her gardens and patios reflected what many of us never saw. If one was to look through a kaleidoscope in brightness—look very deeply—they might just see Marajen Chinigo's one unfulfilled dream. Her name …in lights.

# *Notes*

1     Hughes, Maureen, *An Angry Fire Still Burns.* Illinois: Sunshine Scholastic, 2002.
President James Monroe's description of Illinois in 1818 when he agreed to release the prairie from the state of Virginia.

2     Interviews with Henry Sansone, which took place between June 2005 and July 2006.

3     Interview with Kyle Robeson during May 2007.

4     J. R. Stewart, "Biography of David Stevick." In *A Standard History of Champaign County, 1918.* The Lewis Publishing Company, Chicago, Illinois.

5     Interviews with ex-showgirl, "Star," California, 2005. Star was well acquainted with Marajen Chinigo and Johnny Rosselli early in their relationship.

6     Interview with Bobby Eisner between golf games. Summer 2007.

7     Interview with ex-show girl "T" in an undisclosed location in Las Vegas 2005. Author wishes to note that 'T' spoke on the condition that her actual name not be used. She did say she was under contract at the Sands and Star Dust casinos during most of her career.

8    Interviews with ex-showgirl "T" and a former pimp "Jim" in Las Vegas 2005. Both T and Jim remember Rosselli with Frank Sinatra at the Sands around the time prior to John Kennedy's assassination.

9    Interview with Star' "in 2005. Star remembers being called down to the table after her set where Judy Garland sat with Artie Shaw. "Mr. Shaw said I was great and gave me a $100 tip. You don't forget things like that."

10   Interview with "T" in 2005.

11   Rappleye, Charles and Becker, Ed. *The Johnny Rosselli Story*. Doubleday Publishers, New York, 1991.

12   Interview with Kyle Robeson, 2007.

13   Phone interview with California friend and actress Ms. Barbara Parsons.

14   Dyess, William Edwin, *The Dyess Story*. New York, G.P. Putnam, 1944.

15   Phone interviews with Joe MacNamara. 2007 to 2008.

16   Phone conversation with Bayard Stockton, former CIA and FBI agent, 2006.

17   The Luciano family was well established in the Lercara Friddi province, which was run by Don Vizzini. The story was told to author through a translator from Italy via phone.

18   In 2006 the author spoke by phone with the son of Max Corvo, who had served with Michael Chinigo in the OSS in Italy between 1942 and 1945. Mr. Corvo tried to contact two living people who would remember Chinigo. A short time later the author received a phone call back saying nothing was accomplished. The author got the impression that no one wanted to talk about Michael Chinigo.

19   The story was told to the author by Barbara Main, who was the sister-like friend of Marajen Chinigo.

20   During the research for this book, a California friend and neighbor of Marajen in Palm Springs spoke of this

particular party. The friend, also a long time friend of Rosselli, wished not to be named.

21  Conversation with "T" in California in 2005.

22  Conversation with a former German diplomat, who wished to remain nameless, in 2005. He and his wife were visiting Cuba for "business reasons," as told to author.

23  Interview with "T" in Vegas, 2005. T, who was infatuated with Rosselli, told author that she had never seen that "cold, almost deadly" look from Rosselli before.

24  Rappleye, Charles and Becker, Ed, *The Johnny Rosselli Story*. Doubleday, New York, 1991.

25  Story as told to author by an undisclosed source in Texas, late 2005.

26  The assassination of Kennedy as told in this book follows the information that was relayed to author. Sketchy at best, but these key figures were there and later let the pressure on their conscious speak enough to prove they knew what they were talking about.

27  Interview with "T" in 2005about the fateful date Nov.22, 1963. T believed Johnny and Marajen were at the Brown Derby that evening. T remembers Marajen ordering drinks and no food. When Johnny got up to leave he bent down and whispered something in Marajen's ear, which apparently didn't sit that well. Marajen got up and went to a table where two couples from Palm Springs were sitting.

28  Story told to author via phone in Indiana by an undisclosed source in 2006.

29  Information given over a phone in Indiana by an undisclosed source in 2006.

30  Interview with Steve Farruggia, *News-Gazette* employee for 66 years, in 2008.

31  Information gathered through lengthy phone interviews with two individuals, one in Italy and one in Illinois. The source in Italy is still concerned about repercussions from

certain individuals. The statements from this source were given with the condition that no name be used. I gave my word to protect this source due to the connection with Marajen and the *News-Gazette*.

32    Conversation with law enforcement source from Rome via phone,in 2005

33    Interview with one of Greta Alexander's daughters, in 2006.

34    Conversation with Barbara Main, 2008

35 Phone interview with wife of author Joe Wambaugh. The Wambaugh's were neighbors to Marajen in Palm Springs, in 2008.

36    Phone interview with Lisa Figus who felt Marajen was often taken advantage of by others because of her wealth, 2007.

37    Interview with the professor in Rom,e who befriended Marajen in her later years, 2006.

38    Interview with Joe McNamara, in 2008.

39    Interview with Rita Hirshfeld, in 2005.

40    Interview with former newspaper employee living in Texas. He wishes to remain anonymous, in 2006.

41    A former employee of Marajen's relayed this story to me. The employee was present at the time of the incident, in late 2007.

CPSIA information can be obtained at www.ICGtesting.com
Printed in the USA
LVOW080051150912

298884LV00001B/29/P